ADVANCE PRAISE FOR PHILIPPIANS: A PARTICIPATORY STUDY GUIDE

Bruce Epperly's guide to Philippians brings it all: historical and cultural information, theological perspective, and — most important — encouragement for profound spiritual reflection. Epperly's writing style gently guides readers into an encounter with Philippians, and his discussion questions invite honest and open group conversation. The text concludes with a valuable guide to translations, commentaries, and other resources. I will encourage groups in my own congregation to use Epperly's guide.

Greg Carey
Professor of New Testament
Lancaster Theological Seminary

Many left of center Christians struggle with scripture. It's not just the issue of understanding the text, but rather discerning the spiritual depths of an ancient book. For some the historical-critical study of the scripture has left the text broken into pieces, and thus it is pushed aside. But Bruce Epperly, who is a Process Theologian known for his writings on prayer and spirituality, has produced a study guide that can help such Christians wrestle with the historical-critical issues but then move deeper so as to listen to the voice of God within the text. The format of this particular series, which makes use of the lectio-divina method of reading scripture, is perfectly suited for Bruce's engagement with the text. Having written an earlier volume in this series I believe that Bruce's contribution of a guide to Philippians – a text that speaks of joy from the midst of confinement in prison – is a magnificent contribution that takes the series to a new level. Users of this guide will be blessed – whether they are using it as individuals or in group study.

Robert D. Cornwall, Ph.D., Pastor
Central Woodward Christian Church (Disciples of Christ)
Troy, MI
Author of *Ephesians: A Participatory Study Guide*

Dr. Epperly's guide to Philippians is a great addition to the Participatory Study Series. He brings a different and important perspective that adds to the theological diversity of the series. This guide is great for groups looking delve into Pauline spirituality and the healing joy that Christ brings the world. Reading Philippians in this way will change your life.

Rev. Geoffrey Lentz
First United Methodist Church, Pensacola, FL
Author of *The Gospel According to Saint Luke:*
A Participatory Study Guide

With practical wisdom and inspired scholarship, Bruce Epperly offers an alluring invitation to the the adventure of biblical study. He takes Paul's letter to the Philippians and divides it into 8 manageable lessons that combine spirituality, exegesis, theological reflection, and active embodying of the message. The result is a solid presentation of the historical, sociological, and ideological issues that arise from reading Philippians (and all biblical texts). It is a journey worth taking alone or in a group.

Lisa Davison
Professor of Hebrew Bible
Phillips Theological Seminary

To read and interpret the Bible for oneself is a Protestant prerogative, but to read it well requires reliable guides. Bruce Epperly is an able co-conspirator of the Spirit and the church, leading us through Philippians to find the joy of the high calling of Christ Jesus.

Rev. Dr. George A. Mason, Senior Pastor
Wilshire Baptist Church, Dallas, Texas

PHILIPPIANS

A PARTICIPATORY STUDY GUIDE

Bruce Epperly

Energion Publications
2011

Energion Publications
P. O. Box 841
Gonzalez, FL 32560

ISBN10: 1-893729-97-4
ISBN13: 978-1893729-97-1
Library of Congress Control Number: 2011934737

TABLE OF CONTENTS

THE PARTICIPATORY STUDY SERIES

The Participatory Study Series from Energion Publications is designed to invite Bible students to become a part of the community of faith that produced the texts we now have as scripture by studying them empathetically and with an aim to learn and grow spiritually.

The section Using this Book and the appendices are designed for the series and adapted to the particular study guide. Each author is free to emphasize different resources in the study, and individual students, group leaders, and teachers are encouraged to enhance their study through the use of additional resources.

It is our prayer at Energion Publications that each study guide will lead you deeper into scripture and more importantly closer to the One who inspired it.

– Henry Neufeld, General Editor

Preface
An Invitation
to Adventure

Reading the Bible is intended to be an adventure in which we discover God's presence in our lives and in the world. When we allow ourselves to be transformed by encountering scripture with an open mind and heart, we may be in for a surprise. We might even experience a miracle, an unexpected change of heart reflected in transformed values and priorities in our daily lives. It has been said that people can discover God's guidance with the scriptures in one hand and the New York Times in the other. Today, most of us would add Facebook, Twitter, cable television news, YouTube, and Google as contemporary companions along with prayer and devotional reading in our discernment of God's vision for our lives. For our experience of God to be new every morning, we must take seriously the times in which we live. This was true in the first century, among those who received Paul's first letters, and it is equally true for us who read scriptures online or with our Kindle, Nook, or cell phone.

Recently, I have been pondering the adventure of parenting in light of the birth of my first grandchild. For my young grandson, each day is an adventure in which he encounters the world anew, synthesizing a series of recent memories with the surprises each day brings. Just the other day, he experienced something truly amazing. For the first six months of his life, he'd looked in the mirror not knowing the identities of those who gazed back at him. He was amused and perplexed, and quite interested in their movements, but uncertain about the identity of those whom he observed. One morning, I think he got it. He connected his face with the face in the mirror and recognized the similarity between his grandfather's graying beard, eyes, and movements and the movements projected from the mirror. He laughed in delight and amazement. But, the next day, he seemed to forget the connection and had to relearn it all over again.

The ongoing processes of learning, being surprised, forgetting, and learning again, reflect how we encounter God's revelation in scripture and the events of our lives. Scripture presents us with ancient words grounded in a pre-scientific world view, addressed to people who died more than two thousand years ago. But scripture is also a living word that illuminates our time and place. Scripture reveals who we are and what God imagines for us as God's beloved children. I am convinced that when we read Acts of the Apostles and Paul's letters through post-modern eyes, we can understand the emerging Christianity of the first century and our own emerging experience as twenty-first century followers of Jesus Christ. While Paul did not imagine his letters being read two thousand years later, the ongoing inspiration of the Holy Spirit enables us to "overhear the gospel," to quote Fred Craddock, and discover contemporary guidance from ancient words.

The first century world was a time of pluralism, relativity, and uncertainty. One era was dying and another era was being born. Rome's imperial quest for peace and political unity in the known world awakened people to diversities in culture, lifestyle and religion. The Roman imperial ideology revered Caesar as God's son, who brought peace and order to the known world through conquest and assimilation. In the midst of this cultural and spiritual maelstrom, a small but dynamic countercultural movement arose. Grounded in the experiences of Jesus' first followers, this emerging faith with its vision of a Son of God who ruled through love and non-violence spread rapidly across the Mediterranean world, vying for recognition in the marketplace of ideas and spiritual movements. Though initially guided to some extent by the Jerusalem church and those who had seen Jesus in the flesh, this movement had little organization, virtually no doctrine or ritual, and only a modest hierarchy. Inspired by God, the leaders of this movement were making it up as they went along, trying to determine the core identity of this growing movement, yet affirming fluidity and flexibility of doctrine and practice in its mission to a world of change, pluralism, and relativity.

This young movement had yet to produce its own scriptures. At the time Paul wrote his letters, the gospels were being formed by word of mouth and as they were forming, the early church seemed content with multiple stories, each nuanced in terms of a particular perspective, rather than one uniform picture of Jesus' life and teaching. Only later were some accounts of Jesus deemed more edifying than others, the Four Gospels, and other accounts (for example, the Gospel of Thomas and the Gospel of Mary) placed outside the norm of the growing movement. These new Christians heard the many stories about Jesus along with the Hebraic scriptures (Old Testament) and were, like ourselves, healed and transformed in the hearing.

Today, we can identify with this young movement. For Christianity is no longer the only spiritual option for people in North America. Like the apostle Paul speaking to the Athenian intellectual community at the Areopagus (Acts 17:16-32), we Christians have to form and present our message in a world in which, as the result of the internet and the mass distribution of books, all religions are on equal footing and new spiritual paths emerge with each new day. The recent popularity of Elizabeth Gilbert's autobiography and the subsequent movie *Eat, Pray, Love* gives testimony to the reality that spiritual seekers are just as likely to look for answers in Hindu meditation and devotional practices as in the Baptist or Presbyterian churches of their childhoods. The Dalai Lama is as respected as Billy Graham or the Pope. Like the Athenian spiritual marketplace that Paul encountered, new religious movements abound in our time, and we and our children can mix and match spiritualities, joining Sunday worship with a Monday night yoga class, Quaker silence, Chinese Tai Chi, and Zen Buddhist meditation. Pluralism opens up a new realm of possibilities as well as spiritual challenges for today's Christians as they seek to be faithful to Christ and open to God's world. We can't turn our back on spiritual and theological pluralism, and although we can learn much from the diverse spiritual voices of our time, we must critically and appreciatively encounter them in light of God's ongoing revelation in the scriptures, reason, our faith experience, and the traditions of the churches. Paul's words to the Christians at Corinth – "all things are lawful, but not all things are helpful" (I Corinthians 10:23) – remain wise counsel for Christians today.

Today's postmodernism is not to be lamented, since it reflects the realities of our time: the focus on small communal and personal stories, rather than universally held truths; the emphasis on pluralism, rather than uniformity or homogeneity; and the centrality of concrete experience, rather than abstract doctrine. While we might bemoan this sea change in culture and religion, the postmodern world is filled with possibility as well as threat. Today's Christians, like their first century parents, need to focus on experiencing the Living God, returning to personal and communal witness and testimony, and affirming the reality of a personal God, intimately moving through the experiences of individuals and communities.

We can learn a great deal personally and corporately from Paul's letters. Like today's postmodern Christians, Paul addressed concrete congregational issues, sharing theology appropriate to their immediate needs, and inviting them to experience their unity in Christ in light of the plurality of Christian experience and the pluralism of their environment. Paul spoke to young churches, small but growing in numbers and spirituality, meeting in houses, shops, and sometimes on the banks of rivers, inviting them to experience the God of all people personally and communally. Paul's letters were addressed to communities, first, and individuals, second. Paul had no place for rugged individualism in the "body of Christ" (I Corinthians 12:12-31). Accordingly, what happens between two women in Philippi can shape the quality of life of the whole community (Philippians 4:2-3). Paul saw God at work everywhere, but particularly in the transformation of persons and communities, for whom the Crucified and Risen Christ became the animating power.

This was surely the case at Philippi, where in reading Paul's letter we have an opportunity to eavesdrop on Paul's spiritual guidance to a community that he held dearly. As one who has spent over thirty years in ministerial settings as a pastor, seminary professor, administrator, and university chaplain, I know the challenges of spiritual leadership in congregations, but I also know the bond of love that can unite a pastor with her or his flock. From beginning to end, Paul's letter to the Philippians reflects his deep love for them and his profound appreciation of their support and generosity. They are on the right track but staying on the right track as a religious minority in a pluralistic community is challenging, especially when discipleship is costly. Paul sees God at work in every aspect of their lives and trusts that God's good work will be brought to fulfillment in their individual and community life (Philippians 1:3-11). But, still the Philippians need instruction; they need tutoring in theology and spiritual formation to achieve the harvest of righteousness that God is seeking for them.

Whether in the first century or our time, the realities of pluralism and experiential faith challenge us to be intentional in articulating our theological world view and the spiritual practices that enable us to experience God in our daily lives. I believe that good theology and spiritual practice involve three components:

Vision – a portrayal of the world in which we live and God's relationship to creation. Legend has it that Albert Einstein was once asked "what is the most important question in life?" The scientist replied, "Whether or not the world is friendly." Our vision as Christians involves how we understand God's nature, purposes for human experience, the movements of grace in our lives, our hope in this life and the next, and God's activities in the non-human world.

Promise – the affirmation that we can experience our theology, that is, our vision of the relationship of God and the world in daily life. Faith is lived experience, not just abstract doctrine. We want, as Paul says to the Philippians, to intimately know Christ, not just hear about Christ (Philippians 3:10).

Practices – spiritual disciplines, rituals, or pathways that enable us to experience God's presence and guidance in our ordinary lives. Paul provides a key aspect of his theological vision in his letter to the Philippians, chapters one and two; but in chapter four, especially verses 4-9, he shows how to experience Christ's presence and guidance in the daily lives of persons and communities. The adventure of faith involves the interplay of grace and intentionality. Our spiritual practices or disciplines are ways we open to God's movements in our times and the world. They enable us, with Jacob, to affirm "God is in this place" (Genesis 28:10-17) and with the Psalmist, "to taste and see that God is good" (Psalm 34:8). The joy that characterizes Paul's letter to the Philippians is not accidental, but arises from his intimate heart-felt experience of Christ and his own personal commitment to pray without ceasing so that Christ might be fully formed in his life.

As we begin this joyful adventure with Paul's Letter to the Philippians, I would like to thank Henry Neufeld, my publisher and editor for his support and guidance. Henry provided a vision for this study and gave me permission to work out the details in a way congruent with my gifts as a pastor, teacher, and spiritual guide. I would also like to thank the members of my adult education class at Disciples United Community Church, Lancaster, Pennsylvania, with whom I initially shared this series. I am grateful to Dr. Bob Cornwall who suggested that I write this text for Energion Publications. I am grateful to my former colleagues at Lancaster Theological Seminary, most especially former President Riess Potterveld and former Dean Ed Aponte, whose support made it possible for me to create innovative adult programs, including a prototype for this book, intended to foster spiritual growth and religious literacy in congregational life. As always, I am grateful to my partner in life and ministry Rev. Kate Epperly, D.Min. for her love and companionship over more than three decades – a deep relationship that grows deeper as we share teaching, writing, and grandparenting. For this and all things, I am grateful for God's inspiration and companionship in my pastoral, personal, and academic life.

I am confident of this, that the One who began a good work among you, will bring it to completion by the day of Jesus Christ (Philippians 1:6).

St. Patrick's Day
March 17, 2011

Using This Book
Spiritual Practices for Reading Philippians

The Bible is an adventure book, a library of texts describing God's dynamic call and the creaturely response revealed in the creation of the universe, the history of Israel, and the life and teachings of Jesus and his first followers. Although the Biblical canon, or official texts of scripture, was closed by the fourth century, God is still moving in our world, speaking in our lives in sighs too deep for words, in the cries of creation, and in the affairs of congregations, communities, and nations. God is calling, and all things live and move and have their being in God's creative inspiration (Acts 17:28). Still, we need to pause awhile to hear God's word in scripture and in our lives. We read scripture to know Christ, experience God's presence in our lives, find guidance in our personal and political lives, and claim our vocation as God's companions in healing the world. The Bible is a living document that invites us to become part of God's story "for just such a time as this" (Esther 4:14).

Throughout Philippians, the apostle Paul uses the Greek word *phronein* to describe a certain type of knowledge that embraces head, heart, and hands. When Paul says, "have this mind among you" or "let this same mind be in you" (Philippians 2:5), he is speaking of a unique way of looking at the world, a perspective in which God's revelation in the life, death, and resurrection of Jesus shapes how we experience the world and our relationships. I believe that we need to bring this same holistic knowledge to our reading of the scriptures. Reading the scriptures holistically, integrating mind, body, spirit, and relationships, liberates us from superficial readings of the text and the cultural and religious polarization of our time. When we read the Bible holistically, we can see a variety of perspectives on the text as well as experience scripture as a word addressed personally to us and our congregations. God is still speaking every time we open the Bible. Spiritual practices help us to experience God's vision for our lives, our congregations, and our world.

I invite you to practice the following spiritual disciplines as you read Philippians. You may choose to modify them in ways appropriate to your personality type, lifestyle, schedule, and current personal and congregational spiritual practices. Because most of these practices emerged in agrarian and pre-scientific and non-technological communities, I have updated these practices to reflect our contemporary attitudes toward time and work.

BREATHING THE TEXT

Psalm 150:6 proclaims, "Let everything that breathes praise God." In John 20, following the resurrection, Jesus encounters his disciples and breathes on them, saying "receive the holy spirit" (John 20:22). Breath opens us to the Holy Spirit. Prior to the reading the text, I invite you to close your eyes and simply notice your breath. A focus phrase I often use is: "I breathe the Spirit deeply in and blow it calmly out again" as I let go of any stress or anxiety I bring to this moment of study. Our Jewish parents believed study was a form of prayer. Accordingly, we need to prayerfully prepare for reading scripture. After a few moments of breathing in synch with God's ambient and personal Spirit, begin reading the text, awakened to God's ever-present revelation in scripture and your life. You may discover that scripture is God-breathed and life-transforming when you slow down enough to let God speak quietly through the words of the text.

HOLY READING

As a living word, scripture is always a source of inspiration. Throughout Christian history, and most especially in the Benedictine tradition, persons have come to scripture believing that the Holy Spirit will personally and communally inspire them as they read. Benedict of Narsia (480-547) developed the practice of *lectio divina,* or holy reading, as a way of experiencing God's word as a personal and communal address. Traditionally, *lectio divina* has four steps.

Prayerful Reading. The first step is simply to read the text slowly and meditatively. You may even choose to read it orally, so you might hear the words aloud like the first listeners in Philippi. Savor the words as if you are hearing them for the first time. Don't try to analyze the text or fit it into your previous understandings, but open to God's inspiration in this moment, with as few theological biases as possible. God is still speaking and creating in our lives. Participatory Bible study involves your commitment to becoming a companion with the scripture and letting it shape your experience of the world in the here and now.

Meditating on the Words. The second step involves listening for the words that speak to you personally today. What words, phrases, or images stand out in your reading? What words, phrases, or images console or inspire? What words, phrases, or images trouble or convict you? If you are studying Philippians in a group, you will discover the many ways people can experience the same passage. This reminds us that there is a democracy of revelation in which God addresses us where we are, as persons and communities. Each person, including you, is touched by God and can bring something to our understanding of the text. More than this, this process challenges us to recognize that there are many authentic ways to encounter scripture and that God does not desire uniformity in experience, worship, or theology. (Just think of the variety of ways that Christians have understood the sacraments of the church or the relationship between grace and human effort, reflected in today's "orthodox" denominations.)

Praying the Words. Let the word, phrase, or image soak deeply into your experience. You may choose to repeat the word over and over again, or reflect on its meaning for you today. You may also choose to compose a prayer, based on your encounter with the text.

Contemplating the Words. Scripture often calls us to go deeper and to experience God's personal and creative word in the words of scripture. In contemplation, we choose to listen and then let God speak to us in silence as well as the spoken word. In the midst of busy day, we may heed the words of the Psalmist, "be still and know that I am God" (Psalm 46:10). The God who speaks in sighs too deep for words (Romans 8:26) is constantly inspiring us, speaking to us through scripture, hunches and intuitions, unexpected inspirations, and our daily encounters. While revelation may come as a matter of grace and surprise, we can also prepare to experience divine wisdom when it emerges in the course of the day.

USING YOUR IMAGINATION

Another way to read Philippians or any other biblical text is to use your imagination. This approach, which has become popular in guided visualizations and imaginative prayers, is as ancient as Jesus' parables. For example, Jesus invited his listeners to imagine what it would be like to be a lost sheep or to go in search of a lost sheep on a dark night. He asked his disciples to imagine how they would feel, and what they would do, if they found a buried treasure or lost a precious coin. He asked them to consider the relationship of a father and his two sons, and the joy of welcoming a wayward child home.

Ignatius of Loyola, the founder of the Roman Catholic order, the Society of Jesus or Jesuits (1491-1556), suggested that people use their imagination to find the deeper meaning of scripture. They might, for example, imagine what it was like to be one of the disciples watching the crucifixion of Jesus, by noting the scene, the crowd gathered at the cross, and your own feelings as you watched the Romans crucify your Teacher.

While the Letter to the Philippians doesn't contain parables, you might for example imagine the growth of plant from a seed till harvest time (Philippians 1:3-11) or running a marathon, pressing toward the goal. (Philippians 3:12-16). You might choose to imagine your deepest needs and then experience God supplying them (Philippians 4:19).

AFFIRMATIVE PRAYER

In Philippians, Paul tells us to "think about these things" (4:8). In so doing, Paul is inviting us to embody an affirmative faith by using short phrases to reshape your vision of the world. Spiritual affirmations are statements, positively stated in the present tense, that describe our deepest reality as God's beloved children. Many of us are shaped by negative self-talk. Think a moment: what negative self-talk characterizes your life? For example, I've heard people make the following negative statements about themselves. I've even said a few of them myself. Such statements reveal our sense of inadequacy and inability to live out our vocation as God's children.

– I'm too old to try that activity.
– I'm not talented enough to do that.
– I'm not intelligent enough, healthy enough, or skilled enough.
– I'll never love again, or find someone that loves me.
– I'm too fat, too short, too bald, or too ugly, for anyone to love me.
– I don't have enough time, money, or resources, to succeed.

Our negative self-talk places limits on our lives, which is often reflected in our economic well-being and physical health.

Philippians contains some of the most powerful and life-transforming affirmative prayers. Grounded in his counsel, "Be not conformed to this world, but be transformed by the renewing of your mind" (Romans12:2), Paul reminds his Philippian listeners and us to live by the following affirmations:

- The good work God has begun in your life, God will bring to fullness and it will be a harvest of righteousness (Philippians 1:3-11).
- My God will supply all of your needs (Philippians 4:19).
- I can do all things with Christ who strengthens me (Philippians 4:13).

God wants us to have abundant life in body, mind, spirit, and relationships (John 10:10). Affirmations transform our perspective on the world and open us to a world in which five loaves and two fish can feed a multitude, our love can bring healing to others, and our witness can transform peoples' lives. Affirmations challenge us to move from passive acceptance of injustice and mediocrity to intentional agency to bring health, beauty, and love to the world. They remind us that because "nothing can separate us from the love of God," (Romans 8:38-39) we can claim our vocation as "the light of the world" (Matthew 5:14).

In the course of this study, I will invite you in various places, personally or as a group, to practice *lectio divina*, imaginative prayer, breath prayer, and spiritual affirmations as spiritual disciplines to make Philippians come alive for you.

STUDY RESOURCES

As you share in the Philippian adventure, I invite you to go deeper into the text by using a variety of ready-to-hand printed and on-line resources. You may choose to look at Philippians through the lens of a number of translations. I recommend the New Revised Standard Version, the New International Version, the Philips translation, and the New American Bible as good starting points. Eugene Peterson's *The Message* is a helpful and creative contemporary paraphrase of the New Testament and Psalms.

The *New Interpreters Bible* provides helpful commentaries and discussions of the original text. Bible dictionaries and concordances are also helpful in deepening your knowledge of the original text. Web sites such as Bible Gateway and the Oremus Bible

Browser (NRSV) provide a variety of translations. I have listed a number of solid commentaries in the Appendix. I also commend the following pamphlets in the Participatory Study Series from Energion Publications:

— *What's in a Version?*
— *What is Biblical Criticism?*
— *I Want to Pray*

You can find these pamphlets, aimed at deepening your encounter with scripture, free and in various formats online at http://www.participatorystudiesseries.com.

LESSON 1:
INTRODUCTION AND BACKGROUND

VISION

Participants will gain a basic understanding of the setting, authorship and context of the Letter to the Philippians and its spiritual significance for themselves and its first readers.

They will reflect on their place in the ongoing story of God's good news in the world.

OPENING PRAYER:

Individually or in a group setting, prayer connects us with God and provides the context for understanding Philippians. Study is a form of prayer that enables us to discern and put into practice God's vision for us and the world. In the spirit of Psalm 150:6, we begin with a moment of slow, deep breathing and opening to God's Spirit in our lives.

Breathe in and through us, Spirit of God. Enliven and enlighten our hearts, minds, and hands, so that every breath may be a prayer, drawing us closer to You and one another. In Christ's name. Amen.

READING: PHILIPPIANS 1:1-2

As you begin your Philippian adventure, take some time to read the book in its entirety. Imagine what it would be like to hear these words for the first time as a member of the Philippian community. If you can find the text without chapter and verse notations online (the New Revised Standard Version is on Oremus Bible

Browser, for example), read it as you would a normal letter. You may choose to read the text in one of the following versions: New Revised Standard Version, New International Version, J.B. Philips Translation, or Common English Bible.

In your initial reading of Philippians, look for any surprises in the text. Do you notice anything new? Do you notice any problematic or confusing passages? What do you find most spiritually edifying? If this text were read aloud in your church for the first time, what insights would it provide the congregation in its current setting? Where would it challenge your church and yourself?

In addition to reading the Letter to the Philippians, take some time to read Acts 16, which describes the occasion of Paul's first visit to Philippi. What impresses you about the occasion of Paul's visit? What do you notice about the town of Philippi from the text?

LESSON:

READING PHILIPPIANS

In the ancient world, letters were a luxury and anything but commonplace. In contrast to the immediate internet communication or the overnight or two day service of public and private mail carriers, letters such as Philippians may have taken weeks to travel from source to destination. No doubt, when Paul's letter arrived at Philippi, it caused a stir and was likely read in the community worship service, either entirely in one setting or over the period of a few weeks. Thereafter, it may have been consulted regularly for wisdom and guidance. Eventually the early church deemed it as central to Christian self-understanding and revelatory of divine wisdom for human life. Virtually all letters in the ancient world, including Paul's Letter to the Philippians followed a similar pattern:

1. Salutation, including the writer's and reader's names.
2. A greeting, such as the one with which Philippians begins, "Grace to you and peace from God our Father and the Lord Jesus Christ."

3. A prayer of thanksgiving.
4. The body of the letter.
5. Concluding greeting and farewell.

What do we know about the author of Philippians and the Philippian community to which he wrote?

The scholarly consensus is that the Apostle Paul is the author of Philippians. Internal evidence suggests that Paul was in prison, although there is no clear consensus whether Paul was incarcerated in Rome, Ephesus, or Caesarea. Depending on the location of Paul's imprisonment, the letter was written sometime between 55-62 CE.

Paul saw himself as personally chosen by God to bring the good news of Jesus Christ to the Gentile world. Paul perceived that his encounter with the Risen Christ gave him authority equal to those who knew Jesus in the flesh (I Corinthians 15:3-11). While we may suspect that Paul shared the gospel with his fellow Jews as the occasion arose, his primary vocation was toward Gentiles, especially those described as "God fearers." God fearers were Gentiles whose spiritual lives were shaped by Jewish monotheism, lifestyle, and ethics. Paul was an ardent worshipper and scholar in the Jewish faith of his parents. He followed the rules of his faith as an expression of his fidelity to God. According to his own witness, his fidelity to the God of Judaism was the primary inspiration for his persecution of Jesus' first followers, whom he felt were injecting unhealthy innovations into the Jewish faith.

As I noted earlier, for Paul, everything changed when he had a mystical experience on the way to Damascus. He saw the Risen Christ, received a new vocation and a new life-purpose. He even received a new name, "Saul" of Tarsus became "Paul" the evangelist.

While he did not deny his Jewish roots or assert that God had abandoned the faith of his Jewish parents, Paul's experience of Christ as a living reality transformed him from persecutor of the followers of Jesus to proclaimer of the gospel of grace through a

relationship with Jesus Christ. Paul traveled to cities in the Mediterranean world, meeting with God-fearers and other Gentiles
primarily at the local synagogue and other public places. During
extended visits to the emerging Christian communities, Paul sup-
ported himself as a tentmaker.

Acts 16 describes the occasion of Paul's first visit to Philippi.
Paul's initial visit was guided by the Holy Spirit rather than the maps
of the day. First, Paul and his colleagues experience an unexpected but course-changing message from the Holy Spirit. One even-
ing, Paul has a vision of a Macedonian man, beckoning to him and
saying, "Come over to Macedonia and help us" (v. 9). In response
to this vision, Paul and his companions sail to Neapolis and then
travel ten miles to Philippi, a city of some 10,000 people. Philippi
was a Roman colony located on the Egnatian Road, a major East-
West commercial and military highway. As the name suggests, Philippi was built and named after Philip of Macedon, the father of
Alexander the Great, in 356 B.C.E. Philippi was a Roman colony,
populated by many descendents of Roman officers who had once
served under Augustus Caesar. As a Roman colony, Philippi enjoyed a unique status in terms of government and taxation.

Although the scholarly consensus is that Paul may have visited
Philippi three times, his first visit (occurring between 49-52 C.E.)
was truly a spiritual adventure. Following his course changing vision, Paul and his companions journey to Philippi, where they encounter a group of women gathered at the river for Sabbath prayers
(Acts 16:13-15). As in the case of other Pauline churches, women
were among the first to hear the gospel and took leading roles in
establishing congregations. (See Romans 16:1-16, which lists ten
women as church leaders.) Lydia, a merchant in purple cloth, hears
the good news of Jesus Christ, is baptized along with her household, and invites Paul and his companions to live in her home. Perhaps, the Philippian church worshipped in her home or place of
business.

Conflict seems to follow Paul wherever he goes and Philippi is
no exception! A slave girl, who has the power of divination, en-

abling her to relay messages from the spirit world to human clients
(she would be described as a "trance channeler" in current new age
literature), follows Paul broadcasting his mission, "These men are
slaves of the Most High God, proclaiming to you a way of salvation" (v. 17). Rather than welcoming her free publicity on behalf
of his mission, Paul becomes annoyed and performs an exorcism
just to keep her quiet! This leads to an uproar among her owners,
who lose an important income source, and in retaliation, they bring
Paul and Silas to the local magistrates who have them beaten and
placed in prison, pending trial.

Joy is one of the primary themes of Philippians. Prison cannot
hinder the gospel message or the apostle's joy in Christ's presence.
As Acts proclaims, "Paul and Silas were praying and singing hymns
to God, and the prisoners were listening to them" (v. 25). In the
midst of their prayers, the jail is rocked by an earthquake. Their
jailer, thinking they've escaped, prepares to kill himself, but Paul
and Silas open a new pathway for the gospel by alerting the jailer
to their presence. In response to their faith and personal care, the
jailer and his family accept Christ as Lord and are baptized.

Paul's first Philippian adventure ends with an assertive encounter with the local magistrates. He makes it clear that, as a Roman citizen, he has been treated unjustly and deserves an apology.
The local officials gladly release Paul and Silas and urge them to
leave Philippi before more violence breaks out. After reassuring
the Christian community of their well-being, Paul and his companions travel to Thessalonica, knowing that wherever they go,
God will guide them and that nothing will separate them from the
love of God.

In Paul's Letter to the Philippians, Paul expresses his desire to
see them again. We don't know whether or not he ever returned
to this beloved community. In fact, we know little about the Philippian Christian community of Paul's time, except the following:

1. It was a small spiritual community, perhaps meeting in Ly-
    dia's or another member's home or a local shop. Scholars

suggest that these early Christian communities ranged from a couple dozen to a hundred persons in membership.

2. Most of the Philippians, given Paul's strong comments regarding circumcision, were of Gentile extraction, and were an easy target for Jewish Christian proselytizers.

3. Women were leaders in the Philippian church. In addition to Lydia, Euodia and Syntyche were also church leaders. The conflict between Euodia and Syntyche had serious consequences for the community's well-being.

4. The Philippian community was a small minority in a religiously diverse community. Ruins suggest that Philippi was a spiritual melting pot, where the Imperial religion focusing on worship of Caesar and the traditional Greek and Roman gods were worshipped alongside each other.

5. The Philippian congregation was familiar with diverse interpretations of Christianity. In addition to Paul's grace-filled faith, which honored the Gentile culture, other Christians proclaimed that Gentile Christians needed to follow Jewish ritual practices, in particular diet and male circumcision, to become full-fledged followers of Jesus. Still, as I Corinthians 1:10-12 indicates, the Philippian Christians may have encountered a variety of nuanced Christian messages, each highlighting a different aspect of God's revelation in Christ, most of which were helpful to this emerging community.

THE OCCASION FOR WRITING THE LETTER

Scholars note a variety of reasons for Paul's Letter to the Philippians. First, Paul wishes to thank the Philippian community for their financial and prayerful support. Second, he wants to let them know that despite his imprisonment, he is in God's hands. He also wishes to affirm, despite geography, they are joined in the body of Christ in their joys and sorrows. God is moving through their suffering, just as God is moving through Paul's imprisonment, in order to further the spread of the gospel. Third, Paul is concerned that the Philippians continue to maintain their freedom in Christ, resisting the legalistic message of Christian teachers who require circumcision and strict adherence to Jewish law. Fourth, Paul is counseling them to be united in heart and mind, despite their differences. Following the pathway of Jesus means that they are to humbly serve one another. Humility rather than violence and social exclusivity characterize the Christian lifestyle. The way of Christ differs markedly from the way of Caesar, who was also worshipped as a deity. Christ's peace is based on non-violence and inclusion, while Caesar's peace is based on the sword and subjugation.

The Letter to the Philippians is an example of practical theology, in which the church is called to live the faith it affirms. Paul has a strong sense of divine providence. While God does not control or determine every event, nevertheless, "in all things God is working for good" (Romans 8:28). God is working in the Philippian church and will, through their fidelity, bring God's good work to fulfillment, a harvest of righteousness. God rules the world through loving affirmation and humility rather than power and violence. Unlike Caesar, Jesus Christ does not seek to "lord it over" creation, but seeks to heal and save broken humanity. Christ's path of humble service serves as a model for Christian living. Rather than rugged individualism and self-interest, Christians are called to serve one another, willingly sacrificing so that others might flourish.

Finally, Philippians is an epistle of joy. Paul truly loves this community. He rejoices in their fidelity to Christ and generosity to him. But, more than that, Paul's experience of the Living Christ and God's faithfulness in all things, gives him a sense of joy regardless of the circumstances of life. Whether he is wealthy or poor, free or in prison, living or dying, Paul rejoices in God, and seeks to glorify God by his faithfulness.

OPENING GREETING (1:1-2)

Paul opens the letter with words of humility. Paul and his colleague Timothy are "slaves" of Jesus Christ. While some translations soften Paul's words by substituting "servant," the literal translation of the Greek word "doulos" is slave. It is important to note that slavery was many-faceted in the Roman world. It might involve physical servitude and extreme brutality, similar to slavery in the United States, but it could also involve property and personnel management, tutoring, and medicine. What is essential in Paul's description is that he is accountable to another person; in this case, he is accountable to Jesus Christ. Paul seeks to follow Jesus in word and deed, representing Christ as faithfully as possible to the Gentile world. While Paul's gospel message affirms the importance of spiritual freedom and creativity (see Galatians 5:1), Paul's freedom is grounded in his alignment with God's vision for his life. Paul believes that his mystical encounter with the Risen Christ defines who he is as an apostle of Jesus Christ to the Gentile world. He finds his freedom in affirming, like Martin Luther, "Here I stand, I can do no other." Marcus Borg and John Dominic Crossan are right in their description of Paul's gospel as countercultural. In proclaiming Jesus Christ as Lord, Paul is implicitly placing Jesus ahead of Caesar. Imperial rulers will come and go, but God's Living Word endures forever.

Paul's vision of God's providence expands to include the Philippian church. This letter is addressed to the "saints in Christ Jesus." God's grace has been at work in their lives, presenting them with possibilities and giving them the energy and passion to embody the gospel in daily life. Grace is about connection with God and our willingness to let God's grace flow through us to others in acts of kindness and generosity. God's unmerited grace empowers us to works of generosity and witness.

While it is customary for Paul to salute the recipients of his letters with the words, "Grace to you and peace from God our Father and the Lord Jesus Christ," these words are not accidental. God's grace is the foundation of our faith and through God's grace, we experience a peace that passes all human understanding. Encircled by grace, we can face tragedy and success alike with joy and wisdom.

QUESTIONS FOR DISCUSSION

1. Recently I found a packet of letters, chronicling my relation-
    ship with my best friend over a decade's time. These letters
    reflect our spiritual and personal growth, sense of call, and
    relationships and job situation. In light of Paul's Letter to
    the Philippians, consider your own writing style. Is your
    primary mode of written communication e-mail, text or in-
    stant messaging, Facebook, cards, or letters? How do these
    formats differ? Does the "medium," as Marshall McLuhan
    once stated, shape the message? Do you receive your church
    newsletter over the internet or in paper form? Does this
    make any difference? How do you think Paul's letters might
    have differed if he had the benefit of computers, e-mail
    communication, and social networking?

2. Most scholars recognize that Paul's letters were concrete
    communications to particular congregations and not sent to
    people in general. If this is the case, how does this shape the
    way we read Paul's letters? Should we expect timeless spiritu-
    al counsel or theological reflection? Or, do we need to treat
    Paul's writings as contextual, valuable to us today, but not
    compelling in certain areas?

3. How do you understand Biblical revelation or inspiration?
    Are all the parts of scripture equally helpful or inspiring?
    What parts of scripture, if any, are poetic or metaphorical?
    What parts, if any, should we take literally?

4. If the reading of scripture is also inspired, how do you un-
    derstand God's inspiration of people through scripture?
    Have you ever felt inspired in a new and surprising way by a
    particular Bible verse? How has this inspiration changed
    your life?

5. What do you think of Paul's use of the word "slave" to de-
    scribe his relationship with God? What problems – relational
    or theological –might his use of "slave" create for contem-

porary people? In what ways is this language helpful? Would you prefer the word "doulos" to be translated as "servant?"

6. When you think of the words "grace" and "peace," what images and words do they elicit? What would these words mean to your congregation? If you're congregation truly experienced God's grace and peace as a community, how would this experience change things?

7. Take a moment to reflect on the story of Paul's exorcism of a spirit of divination as described in Acts 16. Following the exorcism, imagine what might have happened to the slave girl? Do you think she might have joined the Christian community at Philippi? How might her life have changed?

EXERCISE

Look up the word "saint" in the dictionary. How might the dictionary definitions relate to Paul's description of the Philippian Christian community "as saints in Christ Jesus?" How do you feel about being described as a saint? Consider what characteristics define saintliness? Are we capable of achieving these characteristics in our daily lives? In what ways might the term "saint" imply differentiation form the world? In what ways does "saintliness" suggest a necessary relationship to worldly things?

THEOLOGICAL/SPIRITUAL REFLECTION

Reread Acts 16:6-10, noting Paul's visionary experience in light of your own spiritual life. According to the Pew Forum on Religion and Public Affairs, 50% of Mainline and Roman Catholic Christians claim to have had mystical experiences or experiences of self-transcendence. The report also notes that 75% of African American and evangelical Christians report mystical experiences. Paul's fist mission trip to Philippi was motivated by his vision of a man entreating him to come to Macedonia. Before that, Paul's mystical encounter with Jesus transformed him from persecutor of the church to prolaimer of the gospel to the Gentiles.

Mystical experiences are foundational in every religious tradition. Should we encourage mystical experiences in the church today? Should one qualification for ordained ministry be the pastor's spiritual life and intimacy with God, described by Marcus Borg's phrase, "spirit person," that is, someone who has a lively sense of the holy and can help others experience the holy? In what ways should we be careful about mystical experiences?

CLOSING PRAYER:

Begin by reading as a group John 20:22, focusing on the words, "Jesus breathed on them and said, 'Receive the Holy Spirit.'" Once again, take a few moments for silence and opening to the Holy Spirit through focusing on your breath.

Holy Spirit, breathe on us and breathe in us. Fill us with new life, so that we may be inspired to follow your way with every breath. Give us your vision and the energy to seek it every encounter. Help us to live each moment prayerfully, sharing the grace we've received to God's glory and the healing of our planet. In Jesus' name.

NOTES

_____

_____

_____

_____

_____

_____

_____

_____

_____

_____

_____

_____

_____

_____

_____

_____

_____

_____

_____

Lesson 2:
A Harvest of Righteousness

Vision

Participants will reflect on the importance of thanksgiving in our relationship with God and one another. They will also consider the nature of God's presence in their lives and the relationship of divine and human activity in spiritual growth. Participants will reflect on the harvest God is imagining for their lives. What fruits of the spirit is God bringing forth in your life? How do you nurture these fruits for the well-being of the community of faith and the world?

Opening Prayer:

In Philippians, Paul constantly reminds his readers and us that joy is essential to Christian life. Joy is not accidental but arises from our sense of God's faithful presence in our lives. Joy and gratitude are intimately related. Gratitude emerges from our sense of the graceful interconnectedness of life. We are constantly receiving grace upon grace from God and our fellow creatures. In silence, take a moment to reflect on the many gifts you have received from God and others.

Holy One, who calls us to live by abundance rather than scarcity, we thank you for the beauty of the earth, the faithful spinning of our planet, the heavens above and this good earth. Give us a heart of gratitude that we may never grow tired of saying "thank you" to our companions and to you, O God, the source of all good things, and most especially your Love that gave us life and your love to which we return at the end of our journey. Let our thanksgiving inspire us to praise and to action as we seek to be your partners in bringing love, justice, beauty, and healing to the world. In Christ's Name. Amen.

READING: PHILIPPIANS 1:3-11

Read the passage at least twice, once silently and once aloud, in two translations, for example, the New Revised Standard Version, the New International Version, or the Philips Translation, and then in a paraphrase or freer translation such as the Message or the New Living Translation.

LESSON

THE GIFT OF GRATITUDE (1:3-5)

Paul begins his greeting with words of joyful gratitude. "I thank my God every time I remember you, constantly praying with joy in everyone of my prayers for all of you, because of your sharing of the gospel from the first days until now." What would it be like to begin the day with the words of the Psalmist, "This is the day that God has made and I will rejoice and be glad in it" (Psalm 118:24)! A sense of gratitude and joy changes everything in our lives. We view the events of our lives in terms of abundance rather than scarcity. We see challenges as opportunities rather than threats because we know that we are not alone in facing them. God is at work in our lives and we can creatively respond to God's vision for us, regardless of the circumstances of life. Beyond that, we are upheld by the prayers of others and the resources of Christian community. Paul believes that we can be spiritually and mentally transformed as we embrace the path of Christ. We can become new creations, living a life of generosity as a result of our perception of God's faithful presence and activity in our lives.

Thanksgiving connects us with God's abundant life and with people whose lives shape our journey. Paul uses the Greek word *koinonia* to describe his relationship with the Philippians. They are bound together as partners by love and faith. In the spirit of I Corinthians 12, they recognize that they are part of one interdependent body of Christ, in which their joys and sorrows are united. Paul recognizes that joy and gratitude are the result of personal and communal stature. One of my professors, Bernard Loomer, stated that "size" or "stature" was one of the primary spiritual virtues. To be a person of stature means that a person is able to embrace as much of reality as possible without losing her or his personal center. It also implies that the well-being of others is intimately connected with our own well-being. A person of stature does not polarize, but seeks common ground with contrasting viewpoints. Surely this is at the heart of the hymn we sang every communion Sunday in my childhood Baptist church, "Blest be the Tie that Binds."

> Blest be the tie that binds
> Our hearts in Christian love.
> The fellowship of kindred minds
> Is like to that above....
> We share each other's woes
> Our mutual burdens bear.
> And often for each other
> Flows a sympathizing tear.

Paul expresses his gratitude for their common faith and united spirit. Philippians is a love note from Paul to a beloved community. His desire is that they continue to grow and he recognizes that an overarching sense of gratitude will deliver them from self-interest so that they might truly experience the love of God flowing through their lives.

GOD'S GENTLE AND PERSISTENT PROVIDENCE (1:6-7)

Paul continues his greeting with an affirmation that is essential to the theological vision of the Letter to the Philippians: "I am confident of this, that the one who began a good work among you will bring it to completion by the day of Jesus Christ."

This section indirectly introduces three theological concepts that characterize Paul's vision of reality in Philippians and throughout his writings – omnipresence, providence, and eschatology. Omnipresence literally means "present everywhere." Paul believes that God moves through every moment of our lives, guiding and sustaining us. Nothing in life can separate us from God's love, precisely because God is the dynamic reality "in whom we live and move and have our being" (Acts 17:28). In terms of everyday life, omnipresence means that wherever you are and wherever you go, God is with you. This concept was brought home in a practical way by a student at Georgetown University, who stated "God goes to Georgetown, too!" These are comforting words for a first year college student, for whom everything is in transition. These are also comforting words as we face the challenges of aging, unemployment, health, and mortality. Whether we ascend to the heavens, descend to the depths, or try to hide from God, God's Spirit is with us (Psalm 139:7-12).

The word "providence" characterizes the nature of God's presence. God's presence in the world is not neutral; God has a bias toward our well-being in body, mind, spirit, and relationship. For Paul, providence does not exclude human freedom and creativity. Indeed, one of the key points of the Christological vision of Philippians 2:5-11 is that God is non-competitive. God wants us to have abundant life (John 10:10). God is at work in our lives aiming at a goal, a harvest of righteousness for us as persons and communities. But, God's goal for our lives shapes, embraces, and enhances our freedom. Providence means that God is moving through all the events of our lives, providing a vision, energy, and guidance so that we might live out our personal and communal vocations. This sense of providence enables Paul to affirm that "in all things God is working for good" (Romans 28), including his current imprisonment.

"Eschatology" describes the fulfillment, goal, or end toward which creation moves. Paul's eschatological vision is both immanent in the here and now and hopeful in light of God's future for creation. Paul is not otherworldly in orientation. Though he trusts the future in God's hands, he also affirms that we live by God's vision one moment at a time. God's "good work" in Philippi involves

God's faithful companionship and guidance in the context of persecution, controversy, and pluralism. The Philippians can't fulfill their vocation alone, but need God's ever-present guidance and grace to creatively use their freedom and agency.

It is important to note that Paul's sense of God's working in our lives is communal as well as personal. God is doing a good work "among" you, that is, in the life of the Philippian community as a whole. Paul's image of the body of Christ joins the personal and corporate, recognizing that no one can be fulfilled unless his or her neighbor and the community find wholeness. Conversely, the health of the community requires the well-being of each part. Paul's words are hopeful to struggling congregations in the first and twenty-first centuries. Regardless of the circumstances, God is working in your community, calling forth its gifts and vocation for service and healing.

A Different Kind of Knowledge (1:8-10)

For Paul, following his Hebraic parents, knowledge was holistic in nature. To know something was to have an intimate relationship with it. So, when Paul in Philippians 3 speaks of "knowing Christ," he implies something more than theological abstraction, but a practical theology that embraces heart, head, and hands. To know Christ is to be formed in Christ's nature and share in both Christ's death and resurrection. In the same manner, Paul prays that the Philippians' "love may overflow more and more with knowledge and full insight to help you determine what is best." Knowledge is not just about information or facts, or the rote memorization of Bible verses, but involves how we view the events of our lives. Do we see ourselves, others, and the world in terms of God's presence? Do we see our neighbor as God's beloved child, regardless of her or his current life situation or behavior? Do we interpret "five loaves and two fish" as hardly enough to feed a family or as the abundant first fruits that will feed a multitude? Do we use our knowledge to support others' spiritual growth and economic wellbeing, rather than gain an advantage over them?

I happen to believe that memorizing Biblical affirmations can transform your life. But, it's not about winning "a Bible drill," but letting God's inspiration in scripture soak in and change the way you look at the world. I must confess that I begin each day with the words of the Psalmist, "This is the day that God has made and I will rejoice and be glad in it." I regularly recite two affirmations from Philippians, especially when I am feeling isolated and without resources to face today's challenges: "I can do all things *with* Christ who strengthens me" (my emphasis) and "My God will supply all my needs." Virtually every time I recite these passages, I feel God's energy and companionship supporting me and calming my anxiety.

God's knowledge, Paul asserts, is loving knowledge. Despite our sinful behavior, God sees us "clothed in Christ" just as God saw a future apostle already residing in Paul's zealous defense of the faith of his parents that inspired him to persecute the followers of Jesus. When we see things "in Christ," we see others, despite their ethnic, cultural, worship, or theological differences, "clothed in Christ" and not our prejudices.

A HARVEST OF RIGHTEOUSNESS (v.11)

God is working in our lives to bring forth a harvest of righteousness. Perhaps, Paul is thinking of the fruits of the spirit (Galatians 5:22-23). He may also be remembering Jesus' parables of the mustard seed (Matthew 13:31-32; Mark 4:30-32; Luke 4:18-19) and the sower and the seed (Matthew 13:3-8, 18-23). Spiritual formation is intended to let the good seed grow into an abundant crop. Paul is well aware that persecution, alienation, and conflict are the weeds that can choke the good seed before it has a chance to flourish. But, he also recognizes that God's providence is at work bringing the good work of personal and communal spirituality to fulfillment. God does not abandon us to our own devices, but God is present in the details of our lives, supporting our growth through insight and inspiration, encounters with teachers and mentors, and the companionship of friends, family, and the worshiping community. Paul is clear that although there are no guarantees in life,

God is nevertheless working providentially within both painful and joyful moments, enabling us to respond creatively and freely.

QUESTIONS FOR DISCUSSION

1) How do you understand prayer? For what things do you pray? Are there any things for which you do not pray? What does it mean to "pray without ceasing" (I Thessalonians 5:17)?

2) In practical terms what does God's omnipresence mean to you? If you believe that God is always present, how might that change your life?

3) In practical terms what does God's providence mean? Do you think God is at work in the events of your life? Where have you experienced God's providential care?

4) Theologians disagree about the nature and extent of divine providence. The author believes that providence is gentle and non-coercive, allowing room for freedom, creativity, and chance. On the other hand, Rick Warren, the author of *The Purpose Driven Life*, believes that God determines all the important events of your life without your consent and that God places certain events in your life to test you and strengthen your faith. Which viewpoint resonates with your understanding of God's work in the world? Do you think God determines everything or is there free play and chance in the events of our lives?

5) In light of Paul's belief that God is working in communities as well as individuals, what good work do you see God doing in your congregation? Where do you see God's grace moving in your church? What are the greatest impediments to God's work in your congregation?

6) Looking toward your own and your congregation's future, what is your hope for your congregation? Where does your congregation need to grow to experience a "harvest of

righteousness?" Where do you need to grow to experience
fullness of life.

EXERCISE

A key theme in this section is gratitude. Take some time this
week and as you begin class to "count your blessings," naming them
one by one. After taking a few minutes to breathe in God's Spirit,
take some time to reflect on those things for which you are thankful:

- In your relationships (family, friends, children, mentors).
- In those whose faith has inspired your spiritual growth.
- In your home.
- In your employment or hobbies.
- In your health.
- In the world – what beautiful things nurture your senses?
  What wonders astound you?
- In your nation.
- In a moment in which God was truly "real" to ylou.
- In a moment in which you experienced grace, healing, or in-
  spiration.

THEOLOGICAL/SPIRITUAL REFLECTION

Philippians 1:3-11 is filled with affirmative prayers. Take a moment to consider the following affirmations based on this passage:

- God will bring the good work in my life to fulfillment.
- I am reaping a harvest of righteousness in my life.
- I give thanks for God's presence in my life.
- I follow God's guidance to discern what is best.

This passage is filled with confidence that God is present in the
small and large details of our lives, guiding us toward wholeness.
Paul's vision of providence inspires spiritual practices such as pray-

erful listening for God's presence. One of my spiritual teachers, Gerald May, described a practice for opening to God's presence in his book *The Awakened Heart*: pause, notice, open, stretch and yield, and respond to God's presence in your life and the world. Lived theology is grounded in our willingness to see the world through the eyes of Christ. Trusting God's providence, take time throughout the day to observe God's presence in apparently everyday events or synchronous encounters. Train your eyes for blessings, inspirations, and God-sightings throughout the day.

CLOSING PRAYER:

In the spirit of this lesson's exercise, pause a moment in silence to give thanks. Then, share moments of gratitude as a group.

Conclude with a prayer of gratitude.

Holy and loving God, who seeks abundant life for us and all creation. Give us the gift of gratitude. Help us to remember always to say "thank you" to you and all of our companions. Let words of praise flow freely from our lips. Let us seek always to bring out the gifts of others, recognizing that as they grow, we are enriched.

May the good work you have begun in our lives grow that we might bring forth a harvest of righteousness that brings abundance and blessing to others. In Jesus' name. Amen.

NOTES

_____

_____

_____

_____

_____

_____

_____

_____

_____

_____

_____

_____

_____

_____

_____

_____

_____

_____

_____

_____

Lesson 3:
Joy in Adversity

Vision

Participants will reflect on the apostle Paul's understanding of God's presence in adversity as well as the importance of Christian unity in a pluralistic age. They will also explore the concept of providence as a lived reality, and not just an abstract theological doctrine. Living worthy of the Gospel involves facing life's challenges with courage and equanimity and seeking unity while affirming diversity. They will also consider the relationship between our responsibilities and fidelity in this time and our hope for everlasting communion with Christ.

Opening Prayer:

Paul affirms God's presence in persecution as well as celebration. Begin this prayer time considering the adversity that you and others are currently facing. Quietly open to God's presence as you pray for those facing challenges of physical and mental health, bereavement, economic instability, and political and social persecution.

Loving God, to whom all hearts are open and all desires known, we ask for your healing touch on all who are facing illnesses of mind, body, and spirit. We ask your blessing on all those who are facing persecution as a result of their faith. Let them find confidence in your nearness, O God. Help us to hear the cries of the poor and become your messengers of grace, justice, and transformation. In Christ's name. Amen.

READING: PHILIPPIANS 1:14-30

Read Philippians 1:14-30 twice, once silently and once aloud, in the spirit of *lectio divina*, described earlier in the text. Let the text soak in as you listen for God's inspiration coming to you in a word, phrase, or image. Quietly open to God's wisdom as you consider the meaning of the scripture and your particular insight for your life today. Prayerfully dwell in silence, reflecting on any inspiration you've received. If you are studying alone, take a few minutes to journal about your experience. If you are studying in a group, take some time for group members to share their insights, affirming the diversity of interpretations of the passage.

LESSON

THE UNHINDERED GOSPEL (1:12-14)

The Philippian congregation is no doubt anxious about Paul's current situation. Will he be released or receive the death penalty? Paul not only assures them that all is well, the apostle has the audacity to claim that his imprisonment has actually advanced the spreading of the Gospel. The imperial guard is now learning about God's salvation through Christ Jesus. Paul suggests that some, like the Philippian jailer mentioned in Acts 16, may quietly have accepted Christ as Savior and Lord.

Paul believes that divine providence cannot be thwarted by human persecution and sin. Like Joseph, whose abandonment by his brothers began a journey that led to political leadership in Pharaoh's court, Paul can affirm "even though you intended to do harm to me, God intended it for good" (Genesis 50:20). God ceaselessly works for our salvation. Our failures and suffering can become the womb of God's new creation. This is good news for persons facing serious illness or economic adversity. Do not give up, God is with you, and your current life situation cannot defeat God's vision for your life.

Paul's words conflict with the spiritual values of his time and our own. Throughout history, prison is often viewed as a sign of personal and social disgrace, yet Paul's imprisonment furthers the gospel message. Further, then and now, many people connect adversity with personal or spiritual failure. Proponents of the "prosperity gospel" assume that if people have enough faith, they will be healthy, successful, and wealthy. Somehow their faith will immunize them from the evils of this lifetime. Conversely, people who are unhealthy or poor must be out of synch with God's will for their lives. Many persons in the new age movement similarly claim that we create our own individual realities, and that negative thinking is the ultimate source of adversity. From this perspective, Paul's imprisonment is the result of his negativity and lack of faith. In contrast, Paul's words to the Philippians implicitly challenge the belief that we are fully responsible for our life situation. With Jesus, Paul recognizes that adversity and persecution may be result of fidelity to the gospel. Good and evil come equally to disciples and persecutors. God's sun shines and God's rain falls on the good and bad alike (Matthew 5:45). But, through it all, God is bringing God's vision toward fulfillment, a harvest of righteousness personally and communally.

THE IRONIES OF EVANGELISM (1:15-18A)

Paul rejoices despite his imprisonment and the ill will that some of his fellow Christians have toward him. Sadly, Christianity has been plagued throughout its history by unbending orthodoxy, leading to ostracism of fellow Christians. Paul notes that some "proclaim the gospel from envy and rivalry, but others from good will." While we do not know the identity of Paul's opponents, it appears that they are using his imprisonment as an opportunity to undermine his apostolic standing, including his vision of God's unlimited and unmerited grace, embracing Jew and Gentile alike. Paul believes even their critiques will further the gospel, perhaps because some people, even among Caesar's imperial guard, will come to believe on account of Paul's critics' message. As the public relations adage goes, "some press is better than no press at all!" God works through the imperfection of God's messengers, Paul believes, to bring healing and inspiration. Perhaps, Paul remembers his own faith journey and where it's led. If God can use Paul the persecutor to be evangelist to the Gentiles, anyone can become an agent of God's grace.

Once again, Paul trusts God to be providentially working through a variety of Christian messages. While Paul would surely fault his opponents for their lack of ecumenical hospitality, he still recognizes that their message may advance the gospel message by bringing people to an experience of the Risen Christ. Now, I must admit this is a tall order. While most of us recognize that unity does not mean uniformity, there are times when we find it difficult to affirm God's presence in those groups whose beliefs, worship style, ethics, or experiences differ from our own. Could it be that Paul is advocating a "big tent Christianity," large enough to embrace progressives, moderates, evangelicals, Pentecostals, and conservatives? Could it be that Paul, for whom theology is very important, nevertheless, places experiencing Christ above doctrinal differences?

In this spirit, I have personally chosen to reframe my theological and political language. Instead of using the terms "opponents" or "opposing" points of view, I use the term "contrasting" points of view or contrasting positions as a way of affirming the many-faceted nature of revelation as well as the relativity of every position in light of the wideness of God's mercy and the immensity of the universe. Further, in using the word "contrast," I affirm that I can grow in my understanding of the fullness of Christianity by embracing the best of differing points of view.

PRAYER MAKES A DIFFERENCE (1:18B-19)

In my childhood home in King City, California, a magnet motto "prayer changes things" greeted me every time I opened the refrigerator door. Today, medical research supports this Christian affirmation. Numerous medical studies suggest that religious commitments, spiritual practices (such as meditation and contemplative prayer), healing touch, and intercessory prayer are associated with better health, positive aging, response to stressful situations, recovery from surgery, and pain relief. Physicists speak of "non-local" or distant causation to describe the fact that particles across the universe can influence one another. Two thousand years earlier, Paul affirmed that the Philippians' prayers made a difference in his ability to face persecution and preach the gospel. While we don't know exactly how prayer works and can never quantify its impact on those for whom we pray, I believe that in partnership with the Holy Spirit prayer creates a field of force that transforms persons' bodies, minds, and spirits. Like the "butterfly effect," described by chaos theory, our prayers – like the flapping of a butterfly's wings in California – can influence the weather patterns in New York and Pennsylvania. Although Paul recognizes that our prayers are not all-powerful, he is clear that they are shaping his own life and enabling him to be more faithful and courageous amid the stresses of imprisonment and controversy. They may even tip the magistrates' decision from guilty to innocent.

Paul believes that our prayers are not just our own; they reflect the movements of Gods' spirit us, connecting us spiritually in healing ways with those for whom we pray.

LIFE OR DEATH? (1:20-26)

It has been said that there are some people who are so heavenly minded that they are no earthly good. This surely is not the case for Paul. In the midst of his current trials, Paul yearns to be with Christ, that is, to experience the fullness of eternal life right now! But, he also recognizes that God is always near and this gives him the confidence and courage to choose life to insure the well-being of the Philippians and the spread of the gospel.

"To live is Christ and to die is gain" reflects Paul's confidence in God's presence and omnipresence. While death would release him from life's burdens, he is equally confident that God is here and God still has a vocation for him. For Paul, fidelity and action in this world is consistent with the belief in the afterlife. In fact, his faithfulness to God in the here and now will contribute to the salvation of others – their well-being now in this world and in God's resurrection life. In light of this, Paul can affirm his hope that "Christ is exalted now as always in my body, whether I live or die." These words echo Paul's counsel to another Christian community, "whether we live or whether we die, we are God's" (Romans 14:8). Paul's strong sense of God's loving providence allows him to face his current situation with equanimity, knowing that nothing can separate him from the love of God (Romans 8:38-39).

LIVE WORTHY OF THE GOSPEL (1:27-30)

Paul clearly recognizes the temptations that the Philippian Christians face, personally and as a community of believers living as a persecuted, countercultural minority. To give allegiance to Christ above Caesar has its costs. No doubt the Philippians are discovering what German theologian Dietrich Bonhoeffer described as the "cost of discipleship." Grace is free and unmerited, but it is never cheap. Its price tag may be a cross or our own personal suffering. The hymn initially sung by Christians in India, "I Have Decided to Follow Jesus," captures Paul's understanding of the potential costs of following the way of Jesus.

> I have decided to follow Jesus…
>   No turning back, no turning back....
> The world behind me, the Cross before me…
>   No turning back, no turning back….
> Though none go with me, I still will follow…
>   No turning back, no turning back.
>   — Sadhu Sundar Sing (1889-1929)

In light of their countercultural faith, Paul urges the Philippians to stand firm and be of one mind. In unity, there is strength. Our shared faith, despite our unique and diverse experiences, enables us to hold each other accountable and uphold each other in prayer and deed. One in the spirit, Christian communities create a synergy that enables us to face trials and tribulations, knowing that God is near and God's resurrection power is ours.

Even now in our time, we can take confidence in Paul's assertion that God is with us and that, in life and death, and celebration and persecution, Christ sustains us. We are resurrection people. But, our lives are also cruciform or cross-shaped. The Risen Jesus is known initially by his wounds, and we too may experience suffering and loss as a result of our relationship with Christ. Still, at the end of the day, integrity, fidelity, and the promise of resurrection life far outweigh any trials of this lifetime.

QUESTIONS FOR DISCUSSION

1. What do you think of Paul's assertion that his imprisonment has actually helped the spread of the gospel? In what ways does suffering strengthen our faith as persons? In what ways does suffering strengthen our faith as communities? In what ways, by contrast, might suffering weaken our faith in God's care?
2. Consider Joseph's affirmation, "you intended to do harm to me, but God intended it for good." Have you experienced positive benefits emerging from negative circumstances? How might you explain this statement to someone who has just been laid off and is unable to find employment or a teenager whose mother has been diagnosed with what appears to be terminal cancer?
3. Paul speaks of joy in suffering with Jesus. Is all suffering somehow connected to Christ's suffering? Is there such a thing as unredemptive suffering, that is, suffering that apparently serves neither personal nor spiritual good?
4. Paul speaks of the importance of prayer in sustaining him in prison. Do you believe prayer changes things? Where have you witnessed the power of prayer to transform minds, bodies, and spirits? Are there limitations to the power of prayer?

How do we theologically make sense of unanswered or par-
tially answered prayers?

5. Paul challenges the Philippians to "live in a manner worthy
    of the gospel." What do you think this means today? In
    what ways are we called to be "countercultural" in North
    America? How do we follow a different pathway than soci-
    ety as a whole? How might this prove to be costly for us?
    Are we willing to pay the price for following Jesus?

6. How do you respond to Christian diversity? Can we remain
    united in Christ while holding divergent beliefs and prac-
    tices? Are others, who differ from us, also faithful to Christ
    and being used by God, or do we merely tolerate them as
    Christians but much weaker or more flawed in the faith than
    ourselves?

EXERCISE

Consider situations where you or others are experiencing
hardships. Realistically look at these hardships and the pain people
– and, perhaps, even yourself – are experiencing. (As I write these
words today, I am at prayer for the people of Japan, who experienced a catastrophic earthquake while I was asleep last night.) Ask
prayerfully for wisdom to creatively respond to these situations.
Ask God to illumine your mind so that you might discover what
sacrifices you need to make to ease others' suffering and provide
them with hope for the future.

THEOLOGICAL/SPIRITUAL REFLECTION

In this session, we spoke about the power of prayer to sustain
and transform people's lives. Prayer is at the heart of Christian
faith. Prayer connects us with God and one another and reflects
our love for one another. Take some time to reflect on your understanding of prayer. When do you pray? What situations elicit

your prayerfulness whether in church or alone? What is your prayer style? Do you include elements such as praise, thanksgiving, and confession as well as petition (prayers for your needs) and intercession (prayers for others)?

If prayer connects us with God, do you believe your prayers make a difference to God, enabling God to be more effective in some situations rather than others? This partnership between God and us seems to be the meaning of gospel passages which suggest "your faith has made you whole." Yet, if we look closely at these stories, they indicate that God, present in the life and healing ministry of Jesus of Nazareth, is always present as an inspiration for people's faith. In the case of the woman cured of a chronic illness – a flow of blood affecting her for twelve years – her faith is completed by divine power flowing from Jesus (Mark 5:35-34). There may be a synergy between our prayers and God's actions in our lives. Our prayers do not change God's love for us or quest for abundant life. God always wants to heal us. Yet, our prayers shape the nature of divine activity in our lives.

CLOSING PRAYER:

We conclude with prayers of intercession and petition. Take some time in silence to consider personal and community needs. Lift up each of these needs in silence. Then as a faithful community, lift up each of these needs, followed by a brief moment of silent soaking prayer.

Holy One, whose vision is for abundant life for all creation. Touch us with your healing hands. Restore us to health and vitality. Give us hope that we might persevere in times of trial and tribulation. We do not always know, Healing Christ, what is best for us or others, but we ask that you be present as our healing companions, guiding us body, mind, spirit, and relationships toward the abundant life you seek for us. In Jesus' Name. Amen.

NOTES

_____

_____

_____

_____

_____

_____

_____

_____

_____

_____

_____

_____

_____

_____

LESSON 4:
HAVING THE MIND OF CHRIST

VISION

Participants will reflect on what it means to have the mind of Christ by exploring the interplay of theology, spiritual formation, salvation, and ethics in Philippians 2:1-11. They will discover the importance of humility, sacrifice, and hospitality in their life as individuals and members of a congregation. Further, they will explore the nature of divine power as sacrificial rather than violent or coercive.

OPENING PRAYER:

The opening prayer begins with prayerful visualization. After a few moments of quiet, read Matthew 5:16-18, focusing on the words "you are the light of the world...let your light shine." Then return to your breath prayer, experiencing God's peace that surpasses all understanding. After a moment, visualize a bright healing light, the light of Christ, described in John 15:9 and Matthew 5:16-18. With every breath, imagine the light of Christ entering you, enlivening and enlightening you from head to toe. With every breath, experience yourself filled with God's healing energy and love. After a few minutes, imagine God's light shining through you giving light to others. Reflect on the following question: Who needs God's light today? Visualize the light of Christ flowing through you to illuminate their path.

Loving God, we thank you for the light of creation giving light to all things. We thank you for your light shining in and through us. Let us be lights in our world, shining like stars to illuminate all we encounter today. Let your light so shine through us that persons might find their way and give you glory. In Christ's name. Amen.

READING: PHILIPPIANS 2:1-11

Read Philippians 2:1-11 twice prayerfully in both a translation such as New Revised Standard Version or New International Version and a paraphrase such as the Message. Prayerfully reflect on what it means to experience the mind of Christ. Consider the following questions: What would it be like to see the world with Christ's eyes and experience the world with Christ's heart? How would it change your life to be guided by the mind of Christ?

LESSON

HAVING THE MIND OF CHRIST (2:1-5)

Paul assumes theological, cultural, ethnic, and spiritual diversity among Christians. But, he also expects that they will share a common commitment to one another and to sharing the gospel, despite their differences. Paul counsels the Philippian congregation to "be of the same mind, having the same love, being in full accord and of one mind." He reminds them to care for their neighbor's interests to the point of sacrificing on their behalf.

One of the key signs of faith is our love and care for one another in the body of Christ. Remember the description of the Jerusalem church in the days following Pentecost: "Awe came upon everyone, because of the many wonders and signs that were being done by the apostles. All who believed were together and had all things in common; they would sell their possessions and goods and distribute the proceeds to all, as any had need. ... [T]hey broke bread with glad and generous hearts" (Acts 2:44-47). Such behavior was countercultural in a world in which humility and self-sacrifice were seen as vices rather than virtues. In Mediterranean society social standing was about respect not sacrifice, honor not humility. People followed the model of the arbitrary and often violent Greek gods, who sought to squash any human display of creativity and power, and the equally violent and competitive ruling Caesars, for whom any show of independence was seen as subversive.

Paul's counsel is countercultural in our society as well. A good place to judge a society's values is by observing its advertising on television or other forms of media. When was the last time thrift, sacrifice, humility, or simplicity were praised as values on a television commercial? When was the last time letting go of status, or what some call "downward mobility," was praised as an example in the media? When was the last time you heard of a company placing people over profits or people giving thanks for paying taxes to provide services for the unemployed or working poor?

In times of economic collapse, we want to hold onto what we have, get ahead of others, and turn our backs on our responsibilities to society's most vulnerable members. This dilemma was brought home to a local pastor a few summers ago. When students register for summer church camps, often the pastor has to sign the form, which includes contact numbers, medical permission, and insurance information. As he reviewed the form, the pastor noticed that the line for health insurance was left blank. He knew the child's family was barely getting by financially. After calling together the elders to get their approval, he placed the name of the church as the responsible party for health care. He and elders were convicted by the gap between their affluence and the child's need, and realized that if the congregation was to be faithful to Christ, it must make certain that every member had health care coverage.

Other Christians have chosen to defer vacations and new cars so that unemployed members of the church could pay their mortgages or feed their families. Over the years, we have chosen to let people facing difficult financial or personal situations live in our home, not as a sacrifice but as a reflection of God's love for us. While our generosity should extend to the stranger and the non-Christian as well as our brothers and sisters in Christ, Paul's words

challenge us to insure, at the very least, that within our congregations everyone has enough to get by even if we have to sacrifice
our lifestyle.

The point I am making is that for Paul, discipleship means sharing in the sufferings of Christ. It also means that we are attentive
to the cries of the poor and see our well-being and theirs as profoundly interconnected. The body of Christ is diseased as long as
parts of the body live in loneliness and poverty.

THE FELLOW SUFFERER WHO UNDERSTANDS (2:6-8)

Theology is profoundly practical for the apostle Paul. In prison, awaiting the verdict that will mean either freedom or death,
Paul has little time for abstractions, irrelevant to the life of faith.
Accordingly, the Christological hymn from Philippians 2:5-11 joins
theology, spirituality, and ethics. It is clear from Paul's other writings that the apostle sees Christ as a cosmic figure, indeed, sharing
in the power and wisdom of God the Creator and in the immann-
ence of the Holy Spirit. Like the author of John's gospel, especially
John 1:1-9, Paul believes that the universe reflects God's wisdom
revealed in Christ. But, the point of Paul's use of what some scholars believe to be a first century hymn to Christ is not primarily the
pre-existence of Christ, that is, Christ's eternal participation in
God's nature, but the affirmation that Jesus Christ reflects God's
nature and character. In other words, Christ shows us what God
is like. Accordingly, followers of Jesus should see Jesus Christ's
self-sacrifice and humility as the model for their own ethical behavior and relationships.

The Christological hymn describes the incarnation as "God with
us." Rather than remaining aloof and distant from the ambiguities
of human life, Christ becomes one of us, sharing in our joys and
sorrows. Two thousand years later, Dietrich Bonhoeffer asserted
that "only a suffering God can save." In his identification with human experience, God's presence in Christ reveals God as "the fellow sufferer who understands" (Alfred North Whitehead).

Once more, Paul is describing a deity whose character is far re-
moved from that of the arbitrary and distant Zeus, whose med-

dling in human affairs is often motivated by injured pride and revenge, and the Imperial religion, represented by Augustus and Nero, both of whom ruled by violence and who had little time for honoring the mundane affairs of humankind. The Lordship of Jesus is gained by hospitality and healing, not destruction and distance. Christ's sovereignty elevates rather than diminishes the value of human life and responsibility.

Philippians 2:5-11, like John's prologue (John 1:1-18), describes what God is truly like. "No one has ever seen God. It is God's only Son who is close to the Father's heart who has made him known" (John 1:18). This is central to Paul's theology and ethics, and as we shall see in the next section, his vision of salvation. There is no theological "bait and switch" here. There is no angry vengeful God hiding behind the loving Jesus. The humble God of the crucified Christ is not changing into the ultimate destroyer at the Second Coming. Paul is clear about the righteousness of God, but God's justice reflects love rather than punishment. The only God we can trust and love bears the character of the Christ, who let go of everything to bring us salvation, healing, and wholeness.

Theology leads to ethics and behavior. The only appropriate response to Christ's humility is to practice humility, generosity, and love ourselves. Spiritual formation involves having the mind of Christ, sharing in Christ's unconditional love and letting go of our ego needs, self-serving individualism, and individualistic pride to serve our brothers and sisters in Christ. We are to imitate Christ by becoming Christ-like, clothed in Christ, and perceiving the world through Christ's eyes.

HUMILITY AND EXALTATION (2:9-11)

Paul asserts that Jesus' humility and willingness to suffer on our behalf leads to his universal exaltation. With the Psalmist, Paul looks for the day when everything that breathes, both human and non-human, will praise God (Psalm 150:6). Paul believes that Christ's impact is universal. Paul's asserts that with the final defeat of death, "God may be all in all" (I Corinthians 15:28). He continues that universalistic affirmation in Philippians: "At the name of Jesus every knee shall bend, in heaven and earth and under the earth, and every tongue shall confess that Christ is Lord for the glory of the Father."

It is important to recognize that Christ's Lordship is universal, and extends even further than that of Caesar, who was praised as ruler of the known world. Christ's reign not only embraces this earth, but includes the deceased as well as angelic realms. God's glory inspires global praise, but it is clear from Paul's differentiation between Christ and Caesar that Christ's reign is characterized by love not fear. Paul believes that even in his glory, Christ's reign is non-coercive and affirmative, bringing healing and wholeness to all creation.

The extent of salvation is a matter of controversy in Christian history and in Paul's writings. While certain Pauline statements focus on the judgment of God separating the righteous and unrighteous, others focus suggest that all creation will be healed and transformed in Christ. Paul proclaims that God will be all in all (I Corinthians 15:28). He also asserts that just as all have died in Adam, all will be redeemed in Christ (Romans 5:12-21). As emerging Christian pastor Rob Bell asserts, "love wins." The passage gives no indication that Christ's self-giving love, humility, and identification with humankind will cease when he is glorified by God.

QUESTIONS FOR DISCUSSION

1. What does it mean to have the "mind of Christ?" What would the world look like if you experienced the world from Christ's perspective?
2. How do you understand the nature of God's power? Does the word "omnipotent" mean that God is responsible for everything that happens, from cancer to tsunami? Is God's power limited by human freedom and creativity as well as God's love for the world?

3. How do you understand the relationship of God and Jesus Christ? Is Christ eternal like God? Do Jesus Christ and God have the same character and way of relating to the world? Or, is there a "hidden" God whose will differs from what we experience in Jesus?

4. When you read the passage, "at the name of Jesus every knee shall bend," what comes to mind? What does it mean to bend your knee to Christ? What feelings characterize bowing to Jesus?

5. What is your vision of the afterlife? How do you imagine heaven? Do you believe that hell exists? On what basis are people saved or damned? Some interpretations of Philippians 2:5-11 suggest that the words "every knee shall bend" implies a universality of grace and salvation. What do you think of this possibility?

6. Take time to read the description of creation groaning in hope of salvation (Romans 8:12-17). What does that say about the scope of salvation? Is the non-human world included in God's healing love?

EXERCISE

Read Matthew 25:31-41 twice prayerfully, considering what it means to see and serve Christ in the "least of these." Take a moment to close your eyes, centering yourself with the breath prayer. Visualize those persons who are the "least of these" in your experience. Try to see Christ in their "distressing disguises" (Mother Teresa) as you visualize them. Ask God for guidance to respond lovingly and effectively to their deepest needs.

THEOLOGICAL/SPIRITUAL REFLECTION

Praise, like prayer, connects us with God. Praise is as much for us as it is for God.

Praise brings beauty to God's experience, but it orients our life toward health and healing.

Mother Teresa said that her mission was to do something beautiful for God in her work with people dying on Calcutta's streets and North Americans suffering from AIDS. Praise brings beauty to God and the world, and inspires care for creation.

Praise reminds us that all good gifts come from God and that we are absolutely dependent on God for every breath and for all of our achievements. But, praise has an ethical component. We are blessed, like Abraham and Sarah, to be a blessing to others.

In your life today, where might praise lead to ethical action on behalf of the human and non-human world?

CLOSING PRAYER:

Take a moment for quiet affirmation of Christ's gifts of grace and love. Note moments in your life when you experienced God's saving and transforming presence. Give thanks for Christ's willingness to share our joys and sorrows.

Holy One, we thank and praise you for blessings beyond counting. We thank you for your faithfulness revealed in the movements of the planets, the warmth of the sun, the predictability of seedtime and harvest, and the healing movements of our immune system. The whole earth is filled with your glory. All things praise you, and so we join with all creation, singing "Alleluia! Alleluia! Alleluia!"

But, most of all, we thank and praise you for your love revealed in Christ Jesus our healer and savior. Help us to trust you, follow you, and serve you in bringing beauty and love to the world you've created and create anew with each day. In Christ's name. Amen.

NOTES

_____

_____

_____

_____

_____

_____

_____

_____

_____

_____

_____

_____

_____

_____

_____

_____

_____

_____

_____

_____

_____

_____

_____

_____

_____

_____

_____

_____

_____

_____

_____

LESSON 5:
SHINING LIKE STARS

VISION

Participants are to reflect what the relationship between God's call and our response, and the interplay of grace and works in Christian mission and spiritual formation. Participants are to consider what it means to "shine like stars," to live by a different value system than the culture around them. Participants are challenged to claim Jesus' words "you are the light of the world" as descriptive of their vocation as God's followers. How would this shape our behavior and our use of time, treasure, and talent?

OPENING PRAYER:

After prayerfully reading Philippians 2:12-14, pause a moment in the spirit of *lectio divina* to consider what these words mean in your life today. What insights are you receiving about working out your salvation with fear and trembling, knowing that God's grace is the source of all good works?

Holy One, you have called us to be your partners in healing the world. Yet, we know how easy it is to be conformed to this world. We know how easy it is to be captivated by materialism and tempted by success. We recognize the ease with which we succumb to divisiveness and polarization. We ask that you give us the inspiration and energy to be transformed by the renewing of our minds so that we might glorify you in the marketplace, the classroom, in the political realm, and in our relationships. Help us to know what is truly important in life and by our values give light to the paths of our neighbors. In Christ's Name. Amen.

READING: PHILIPPIANS 2:12-3:1A

Read Philippians 2:12-3:1a quietly and prayerfully in a translation of your choice. In your second reading, note the times Paul uses the word "rejoice" or "joy" in the text. Consider the meaning of rejoicing in Christian life and in your own life. What does joy have to do with fidelity to countercultural Christian values?

LESSON

CALL AND RESPONSE (2:12-14)

Paul is widely considered to be the apostle of grace. For Paul, all that we are and can achieve comes as a result of God's unconditional grace. We cannot earn our salvation; salvation and healing come as a free and unmerited gift from God through Jesus Christ our Savior. Paul's theology is often contrasted with the Letter of James, which asserts that faith without works is dead (James 2:14-17). Philippians 2:12-14 suggests that there is common ground in Paul's and James' understanding of the relationship of human effort and divine initiative.

At first glance, the words "work out your salvation with fear and trembling" seem antagonistic to Paul's understanding of grace. They imply that our agency is essential to our well-being now and in the afterlife. While Paul proclaims the priority of grace in the Christian life, Paul is not denying human agency and creativity, nor is he assuming we are puppets whose actions are determined solely by God. Rather, we are responsible for our behavior and our well-being and our congregation's mission is partly in our hands.

Salvation, for Paul and the early Christians, has at least two meanings. On the one hand, similar to the Jewish word "shalom," it means peace, wholeness, and health of mind, body, spirit, and relationships. What we do in terms of caring for ourselves and others truly makes a difference. To be saved means to be healthy in mind, body, spirit, and relations. In this context "fear and trembling" does not mean anxiety as much as the recognition that life is serious business and that our values and actions have an impact on our lives and the lives of others – spouses, children, friends, church, and society. You can catch this same spirit in the words of former slaveholder John Newton's "Amazing Grace." In light of his own personal transformation due to a wholly unmerited encounter with the Living Christ, Newton penned, "Twas grace that taught my heart to fear and grace my fears relieved."

Following Christ means active efforts to transform the world not passive acceptance of the status quo. For Paul, faith, grace, and works are interconnected. As Luther was to put it, we are called to be little Christs – blessed to be a blessing – who actively share the grace we've received with others.

Paul balances the focus on works with his recognition of the priority of grace. Paul asserts that "it is God who is at work in you, enabling you both to will and to work for his good pleasure." In the spirit of John Wesley, grace is prevenient or prior to any of our efforts. In a dynamic and ongoing process, God calls and we respond. God begins the good work and nurtures us on the pathway toward a harvest of righteousness.

God's working in our lives will always be mysterious. In light of Paul's mystical sense of Christ in us or our living in Christ, we can imagine God as the inner source of insights, inspirations, and nudges and the energy to achieve them. The Spirit is always interceding and inspiring us with sighs too deep for words. Spiritual practices enable us to claim the grace that inspires us.

A DIFFERENT STANDARD (2:14-18)

Paul counsels the Philippians to live by a different ethical and behavioral standard than their neighbors. As Stanley Hauerwas and William Willimon counsel, Christians are called to be "resident aliens," living in the world, but not being conformed to the world's value system.

"Don't grumble," Paul counsels. Grumbling or complaining disrupts community life by its focus on what I want and my ego needs without regard to the health of the community. In this short passage (Philippians 2:12-3:1a), Paul uses the word "rejoice" five times. Joy is antithetical to grumbling. Joy expands our world, grumbling contracts our experience, so that we think no further than our own interests or problems. Joyful living involves losing our lives and letting go of our ego's needs so that we might experience the hospitable and spacious mind of Christ. While joy may lead us to challenge the status quo and the injustices of the world, joy has no enemies. Like Paul's concept of love, described in I Corinthians 13, joy is patient and kind, not arrogant, boastful, arrogant, or rude. Joy does not "insist on its own way; it is not irritable or resentful; it does not rejoice in wrong doing but rejoices in the truth" (v. 4-6). Joy trusts that God's larger vision of our lives and the world will win the day and that our efforts at going from self-interest to sacrificial living are sustained by a love that never ends.

As the campfire song proclaims, "They will know we are Christians by our love." This is what it means to shine like stars in the sky. Recently, I have begun the practice of "blessing" people wherever I go. When I bless people, I quietly wish them joy, happiness, and well-being. I share the blessings I have received, whether in a smile, a kind word, letting someone go ahead in line, or simply saying a prayer for them. Blessing has changed my world. I now see others through the eyes of joy. Surprisingly, when I bless others, I discover that I have more time, money, and energy than I expected. I let go of control and open to God's vision for my life and relationships. Blessing isn't easy, I've discovered, for often fear, judgment, and anger get in the way, and I have to call myself back to God's vision of Shalom and my calling to be God's partner in blessing and healing the world. I have to remind myself that God calls me to be the light of the world – "this little light of mine," as the song says, can bring God's love to a room, a person, a family, a church, or a community.

PARTNERS IN MISSION (2:19-3:1A)

Paul's mission depends on the loyalty and support of his partners in ministry. Ministry is a corporate enterprise. Spiritual leaders need both the prayers and commitments of a team of spiritual
companions. One of Paul's closest associates was Timothy. Paul
was Timothy's teacher and mentor. A Greek (Gentile) by birth,
Timothy was nurtured in a Christian household by his mother and
grandmother (II Timothy 1:5). As a Gentile, Timothy would no
doubt have immediate rapport with members of the Philippian
church. Paul trusts Timothy to be his emissary to Philippi to share
information about his situation in prison and relay his written and
oral counsel.

Epaphroditus is a child of the Philippian church. It is likely that
he accepted Christ as his Savior during one of Paul's visits to Philippi. Paul had nurtured him in the faith and acknowledges his importance by referring to him as "my brother and co-worker and
fellow soldier." It is likely that Epaphroditus was responsible for
bringing the Philippians' gift to Paul. In the course of his service
to Paul and the gospel, Epaphroditus became gravely ill, causing
great anxiety to his friends in Philippi. We can suspect that Paul
has sent him home to reassure the Philippians as to his well-being
and to deliver the epistle. On a pastoral level, Paul as the Philippian church's founding pastor is affirming Epaphroditus' emotional needs – home is where the heart is and coming home will restore
his spirit as well as his health. Pastoral ministry at its best cares for
persons as much as projects, and Paul knows that Epaphroditus'
return to Philippi will bring joy to his colleague and further the
aims of the gospel.

QUESTIONS FOR DISCUSSION

1. Consider Paul's statement, "Work out your salvation with
   fear and trembling." At first glance, and apart from context,
   what might these words mean to you? What "works" does

God call you to do? In what way does our agency in nurturing healthy relationships at home, church, and the community contribute to your salvation?

2. Paul uses the words "fear and trembling" as if to say that what we do matters and can have serious consequences. In what ways might you as a Christian live by a different value system than the surrounding culture? How might this shape your generosity to others? How do our behaviors make a difference to others?

3. Paul asserts that "God is at work in you." What do you think it means to say God is working in your life? Where have you identified God's guidance, vision of possibilities, or energy moving in your life? What might God be calling you or your congregation to do in the future? What gifts do you see God giving your church to help it live out its vocation?

4. Paul challenges the Philippians to "do all things without murmuring?" What do you think he means? When do you murmur or complain? Where do you see murmuring in the church? How does that contribute to the atmosphere of the community and interpersonal relationships? How might you address conflicts or differences in style without murmuring?

5. What does it mean to "shine like stars in the world?" How might you shine for God at home? At the workplace? In your social or political relationships?

6. Paul speaks of his close co-workers Timothy and Epaphroditus. Who have been your mentors? Who has helped you on your spiritual journey? Where do you need to help your spiritual leaders fulfill their calling?

EXERCISE

Throughout the day, make a commitment to "bless" people by your thoughts, words, and deeds. Notice the difference it makes in your life to see yourself as an agent of God's blessing. Notice the responses that others give to you when you bless them, even if your blessing is only a simple act of courtesy or silent prayer or a word of recognition to the checkout clerk.

THEOLOGICAL/SPIRITUAL REFLECTION

Grace is central to Paul's theology. Paul believes that God's grace embraces and empowers us regardless of the past or our ethnicity, theological position, ethics, or lifestyle. Grace is freely given, and can never be earned. Grace must simply be accepted as an act of faith.

Yet, for some Christian leaders, faith itself becomes a require-ment of receiving God's grace, that is, faith becomes something we must do for God to love us. Faith, then, becomes a work, a way of earning God's love. The focus on faith as a human achievement necessary for salvation often emerges when people are told that they must believe certain things or participate in certain rituals to receive God's love. Others are told that if they have questions or challenge traditions of the faith, they will be judged as unfaithful and disobedient.

The relationship between faith and grace is subtle and complex. Grace inspires us to believe and to do good works. Prayer opens us to God's presence. But, God is already here, seeking our well-being long before we have sought God's presence. Grace, accord-ingly, does not depend on our faith, but faith opens us to receive the fullness of God's love in our life. Faith opens us to new dimen-sions of life and greater influxes of God's ever-present power in our livers. Noted preacher, Ernie Campbell once noted that "there are only two kinds of people in the world. Those who are in God's hands and know it, and those who are in God's hands and don't." Faith enables us to experience ourselves, even in our imperfections and doubts, as being in God's hands now and forevermore. We don't earn our place with God; it flows from God's ever-abundant love revealed in the grace of Jesus Christ and the inspiration of the Holy Spirit.

CLOSING PRAYER

Begin this time of prayer with quiet reflection about where God is working in your life. Reflect on your personal "God-sightings" and their meaning for your spiritual maturity and care for others. Ask God in the silence to give you guidance to find the pathway to fulfilling your vocation as God's beloved child.

Loving God, who is constantly working in our lives, show us your way. Work through our efforts so that together we might do something beautiful. Awaken us to our gifts for service and give us energy and direction for the path ahead. Help us always and in all things to be faithful to you. Illuminate us and our freedom and creativity so that we might shine like stars in the heaven for your glory and the well-being of my companions. In Christ's name. Amen.

NOTES

_____

_____

_____

_____

_____

_____

_____

_____

Lesson 6:
No Second-Class Christians

Vision

Participants will reflect on issues of legalism and grace in Christian experience in light of Paul's critique of the circumcision party. Participants will consider the essential equality of all Christians and the importance of affirming Christian diversity.

Opening Prayer:

Begin by taking a moment to reflect in silence on the diversity of Christian experience and the importance of many voices in the formation of a vital and holistic faith. As a group, lift up the varieties of Christian experience and their unique gifts. Take a moment to give thanks for God's personal relationship with all creation and God's intimate care and inspiration for each one of us.

Holy One, whose love and creativity, brings forth life in all its diversity. We give thanks for your presence and activity in the many voices of faith and in spiritual leaders throughout the centuries — Augustine, Luther, Calvin, Zwingli, Wesley, Williams, Dorothy Day, Billy Graham, Martin Luther King, and Mother Teresa. We are grateful that you love each one of us as if there is only one of us, and that you are constantly inspiring us. Help us, O God, to honor diversity of experience, worship, theology, and mission. Help us to learn from the many faces of Christian faith and practice. In Christ's Name. Amen.

READING: PHILIPPIANS 3:1B-11

Read Philippians 3:1b-11 twice. On your second reading, circle the words that stand out. Consider their importance in the passage and their meaning for you today. What is the relationship of faith and works? Do we have to do something "extra" to receive God's love?

LESSON

FIGHTING WORDS (3:2-4)

Paul's letter takes a radically different tone at Philippians 3:2. Gone is the peacemaker, replaced by a theological street fighter. The difference in attitude and tone has led some commentators to see this as a separate letter, later inserted into the body of the text. However, a majority of commentators see Philippians as either one complete letter or see the possibility of multiple letters as unsettled and a matter of indifference. In any event, in the process of canonization, or compiling the New Testament books, the Letter to the Philippians as a whole was considered inspired and essential in Christian formation.

"Beware of the dogs, beware of the evil workers, beware of those who mutilate the flesh!" While there is no certainty as to the objects of Paul's angry words, many commentators believe they are directed to Jewish Christians who taught that Gentiles must first follow Jewish rituals, including male circumcision, to be fully Christian. A personal relationship with Jesus was not enough in their eyes to warrant the title "Christian." A Gentile needed to become, for all intents and purposes, a Jew and, thus, renounce one's own ethnicity and culture, to become an authentic follower of Jesus. Paul addresses this issue directly in Galatians, but obviously the same issues are at work in Philippi as well.

For Paul the issue is two-fold: 1) the status of Gentiles as members of the Christian community and 2) the relationship of grace, faith, and works. As apostle to the Gentiles, Paul affirms that God's grace is universal and freely-given. God's grace includes all persons, regardless of ethnicity and race. Just as all have sinned and fallen short, Jew and Greek alike, all are equally welcomed into God's realm. To place certain requirements on Gentiles would fracture our unity in Christ and place them in the category of second-class Christians, who must do something extra to receive God's freely given grace. If we must do something extra to receive God's grace and our place in the community of faith, then the grace of God is nullified and is dependent on our achievements. In practice, then a person will never know if he or she has done "enough" to receive God's grace and promise of salvation in this life and the next. While Paul recognizes that grace leads to action, our ethical actions and religious practices do not earn God's love. God loves us because we are God's beloved children, regardless of our sin and brokenness.

From Paul's perspective, faith is our acceptance of God's love and willingness to trust God with the whole of our lives, both our imperfection and achievement. Faith always includes an "in spite of" element, that is, we can never fully fathom God, on the one hand, and our faith is always limited and imperfect, on the other hand. This "in spite of" aspect of faith is captured by a conversation author Madeleine L'Engle had at one of her lectures. In the question and answer period after a talk, a student asked her, "Do you believe in God without any doubt?" To which the author responded, "I believe in God with all my doubts."

Paul asserts that Jews and Gentiles alike need God's grace. We are all on equal footing as God's beloved children, who have fallen short of God's vision for our lives. God's love embraces all of us, regardless of ethnicity or culture.

A HEBREW AMONG HEBREWS (3:4-6)

Paul's critique of the legalism of Jewish Christians is not to be confused with anti-Judaism. As Romans, chapters 9-11, clearly asserts, God's covenant with the Jewish people stands firm. While

Christ, according to Paul, fulfills the law and stands as the fulfill-ment of the Jewish spiritual tradition, God is still at work in Juda-ism. God is faithful. God never forsakes God's people or promises. God's promises endure forever. This is good news for Gentiles: if God breaks the covenant with the Jewish people, how can we de-pend on God's promises to us?

To strengthen his case, Paul states his credentials. He believes that he surpasses all his theological critics in following the law of Moses and the Jewish people. He has done everything right in terms of the tradition's rules, and his fidelity to the God of his people led to his persecution of the Jesus' movement. Then, everything changed. Paul experienced the Risen Jesus on the road to Damascus. His mystical experience transformed his life and gave him a new mission, to share the Risen Jesus with the Gentile world.

OLD CREATION AND NEW (3:7-9)

From his own experience of personal transformation, Paul pro-claimed that if anyone is in Christ, he or she is a new creation (II Corinthians 5:17). For Paul, the new creation he experienced in Christ transformed his value system. His previous religious exper-iences no longer satisfied him in light of knowing Christ. He de-scribes them as "rubbish" or, more strongly, "dung." Once again, Paul is not denying God's presence in the faith of his fathers and mothers. God's covenant with the Jews continues. But now Christ is everything and all-sufficient. Like the person who sells everything to purchase the pearl of great price, Paul sacrifices everything to share in Christ's death and resurrection.

KNOWING CHRIST (3:10-11)

"I want to know Christ." For Paul, knowing Christ involves more than information or abstract theological doctrines about Christ; it involves an intimate connection in which Christ becomes the an-imating center of our lives. Paul speaks of "Christ in me" and "Not I but Christ" to describe a mystical sense of Christ's nearness, as close as the air we believe.

For most of us, the closest analogies might be the intimacy of marriage, spiritual friendship, and parenting, in which we are in synch with our loved one, connected spiritually as one mind and heart. In such a relationship, we literally can't live without the other, and we would sacrifice time, talent, and treasure, and even our life itself that our beloved might life.

Christ is the life-transforming energy in all things and when we draw near to Christ through the spiritual practices Paul describes in Philippians 4:4-9, we will become new creations, formed by Christ's spirit and committed to Christ's work.

QUESTIONS FOR DISCUSSION

1. Where have you experienced "legalistic" religion? In what ways are rules helpful in the life of faith? In what ways can they be destructive?

2. One of Paul's issues is the affirmation of Gentiles as first class Christians equal to the Jews in relationship with God. Have you ever experienced persons or religious groups treated "second class?" Have you ever heard of Christians being treated "second class" by other Christians? On what basis was this judgment made? What impact do such judgments have in the life of the church and relationships among Christians?

3. In the life of faith, should our rules ever be flexible? In what ways do you see flexibility in Jesus' response to others?

4. Paul speaks of his previous life, despite his faithful following of the law as "trash." Have you ever experienced leaving one way of life to embrace another? Why did you leave the previous life? What was "good" about the previous life? What did you gain in embracing a new life?

5. After reading Philippians 3:7-11 aloud as a group, gather in small groups to discuss the following questions, then return to the large group for further conversation.

a. What do you think Paul means when he says his goal is to "know Christ"?

b. When have you experienced Christ in a deep and meaningful way?

c. What practices have been most helpful in nurturing your experience of Christ?

EXERCISE

Once again, we begin with a breath prayer. After a few minutes of prayerful breathing, invite Christ to enter your life with each breath. Feel Christ's inspiration, healing energy, and mission filling you. As you exhale, let go of anything that stands between you and fulfilling Christ's mission in your life.

In the stillness, take time to follow the principles of Matthew 7:7-8: "ask, search, knock." Ask Christ to reveal to you his mission for you in your time and place. Ask Christ to give you the courage, persistence, and energy to fulfill the many missions he envisages for your life.

THEOLOGICAL/SPIRITUAL REFLECTION

Knowing Christ is at the heart of Christian faith. It involves having the "mind of Christ" and seeing the world with Christ's eyes and letting Christ's vision guide your decision-making.

In knowing Christ, you become a little Christ (Martin Luther), giving and receiving Christ in every situation and encounter.

Meditate a few minutes on Albert Schweitzer's concluding words to *The Quest for the Historical Jesus*.

> He comes to us as One unknown, without a name, as of old, by the lakeside, He came to those men who knew him not. He speaks to us the same word: "Follow thou me!" and sets us to the tasks which He has to fulfill for our time. He commands. And to those

who obey Him, whether they be wise or simple, He will reveal Himself in the toils, the conflicts, the sufferings which they shall pass through in His fellowship, and, as an ineffable mystery, they shall learn in their own experience Who He is.

Knowing and following are two sides of the same experience. Take time to meditate on Jesus' words to the men and women who became his disciples: "Follow me." What does this invitation mean for you today? What does it mean to your congregation as it seeks to life out Christ's mission the social, economic, cultural, ethical, and religious complexities of our time?

Over a hundred years ago, the characteristics of Charles Sheldon's *In His Steps* made a commitment to ask for God's guidance whenever they made a decision. "What would Jesus do?" animated their decision making. Since then, in ways that join both humor and serious reflection, others have asked, "What would Jesus drive?" or "What would Jesus eat?" or "What would Jesus purchase?" While there aren't always precise answers to such questions, they invite us to become spiritually aware, recognizing that we are always on holy ground, meeting Jesus in every encounter.

CLOSING PRAYER:

Holy One, help me to know you. Help me to see your face in the tangled web of life.

Help me to follow you rather than the crowd – walking your path even if it means going against social convention and self-interest. Help me to give my ultimate allegiance to you rather the Caesars of our time – whether in politics, business, economics, or ethics.

Let me see with your eyes and act with your hands in Christ's Name. Amen.

NOTES

LESSON 7:
EYES ON THE PRIZE

VISION

Participants will reflect on what it means for them to put Christ first in their lives, pressing toward the goal of God's reign, salvation, and wholeness. They will also consider the role of imitation or spiritual modeling in attaining spiritual maturity.

OPENING PRAYER:

Begin with photos or other media of persons running the races of life (for example, an excerpt from Chariots of Fire, the Special Olympics, a mountain climber, an elderly couple walking together, a marathon runner). Let these invite us to consider the race that we are running as followers of Christ. What are the challenges and obstacles? What is our hope at the end of the race?

Holy One, whose energy moves through all creation. We thank you for being alive today, for waking up this morning, and for the challenges of running the race of faith.

We are grateful for parents in the faith – Mary and Joseph the parents of Jesus, Peter and Paul, Mary of Magdala and Lydia of Philippi – and for little known persons who showed us what it means to be a follower of Jesus – parents, Sunday school teachers, pastors, spiritual guides, friends in the faith, spouses. We pause a moment to name our cloud of witnesses. (Name those who shaped your faith.) Most of all, we thank you for Jesus of Nazareth, our savior and friend, who revealed to us the love of God and the path we are called to follow. We thank you, Jesus, for all that you have been and all you will be as we run the race of faith. Guide our feet,

O God, that we may run with strength, courage, persistence, and energy. And, that every day, we will praise and give you glory for our wondrous life and calling. In Christ's Name. Amen.

Reading: Philippians 3:12-4:1

Read Philippians 3:12-4:1 in translation form such as New Revised Standard Version, New International Version, or the Barclay or Philips translation along with a paraphrase such as the Message or the Living Bible.

Lesson

Running the Race of Faith (3:12-16)

After asserting his qualifications as a Jewish teacher and a Christian apostle, Paul steps back, perhaps recognizing his need to make a connection with his audience. His words might, at first glance, appear to be boastful and place him in an entirely different spiritual world than his listeners. Paul is not perfect, he admits. Despite his mystical experiences, his call to be apostle to the Gentiles, and his leadership in the church, Paul – like his listeners - is still growing in faith. The journey of faith is a process and not a destination. We are going and growing from glory to glory in the process of spiritual growth and sanctification.

Stephen Covey once counseled that we should begin with the end in mind. Without a vision, people, congregations, and nations lose their way and dreams perish. With a vision, we know where we are heading, even if we don't know the exact route or the challenges on the way.

Looking toward the goal of the heavenly calling in Christ – the harvest of righteousness – Paul discovers the difference between what is essential and what can be sacrificed for the greater good, the goal God has in store for us.

"Forgetting what lies behind, straining forward to what lies ahead" is essential to spiritual, emotional, and relational health. There are times we need to let go of the burden of the past – the times we've been hurt, our anger toward parents and employers, the scars of childhood. This isn't always easy and requires forgiveness as well as the support of trusted friends and at times counselors and pastors. We may also need to let go of past achievements, even good things (for example, Paul's achievements as a Jewish teacher or long-held beliefs) to embrace the horizons of God's new creation. "Press onward" persistently and with courage, Paul advises, as you venture from the familiar world and comfort zones toward the horizons of God's future. The scriptures describe a holy adventure in which people were called to let go of the past to claim God's vision for their lives – Abraham and Sarah leaving their hometown to God to seek a promised land, Esther claiming her role as queen in terms of her Jewish ethnicity rather than remaining silent in a time of threat, Peter launching out to fish in deeper waters, and Paul's willingness to follow a vision, changing his plans to go to Philippi.

Spiritual health involves breaking with the past, even the traditions that nurtured us as children. Peter has a dream to eat unclean food and learns that God's salvation and revelation extends to formerly unclean Gentiles. Paul encounters Christ and chooses to let go of his previous faith practices to embrace new life in Christ. The Protestant reformers proclaimed "the reformation is always continuing" and that is our calling today. Paul's words challenge us to ask: What new thing is God calling us toward? What baggage do we need to jettison to claim God's new pathways for our lives?

IMITATION, MENTORING, AND SPIRITUAL GROWTH (3:17)

Harry Chapin's "Cat's Cradle" describes the relationship of a father who neglects his child to pursue his business career. Over the years, his son observes him, picking up his own values from the values and priorities embodied by his father. The song ends with the son excusing himself from visiting his now retired father, noting the challenges of work and family. The father laments that his son grew up to be just like him. Imitation occurs naturally in the life of a child. My six-month-old grandson is at this very moment watching me typing on the computer. My tasks are at the moment more interesting to him than his toys. My own son, now a father, is imitating my behavior as his father – he spends time with his son every morning before he goes to work. I suspect in the years to come he will read with his son in the morning and at bedtime just like I did when he was a child along with teaching him to play baseball, ride a bike, and play basketball.

Paul counsels the Philippians to imitate his spiritual practices and values in the way that Paul is imitating Christ. Paul places his relationship with Christ and his humble commitment to promoting spiritual well-being and unity in the Philippian church as his highest value. They are to look to Paul and glimpse what it means to follow Christ in Christian community. Like Paul, they are to press toward the goal of Christ's salvation, suffering and rising with their Savior.

Paul's understanding of spiritual imitation is not narcissistic or coercive. Paul is a strong proponent of diversity (I Corinthians 12) but he also recognizes that the greatest of gifts is love in which otherness leads to unity and holiness. Mentoring in the Christian life is about helping less mature Christians discover their vocation as Christ's disciples. Faithful mentoring, like good parenting, gives a person both "roots and wings," a strong spiritual and emotional foundation that enables one to embrace her or his own unique callings in life. Mentoring is a holy vocation because it helps people grow in wisdom, stature, and faith.

THE FIGHT GOES ON (3:18-4:1)

Joy is the heart of Paul's message to the Philippians. Joy is a sure sign of our relationship with God. But, Paul also recognizes that joy comes from trusting God and avoiding theological and ethical pitfalls. He tells the Philippians to beware of those whose God is their belly. Commentators are uncertain of the identity of the objects of Paul's concern. On the one hand, some commentators identify them with the Jewish Christians cited earlier in the chapter, for whom entry into the Christian faith requires strict observance of Jewish rituals and diet. On the other hand, other commentators suggest that Paul is referring to the spirit-filled libertines, criticized in I Corinthians, who believed that their spiritual experiences freed them from all constraints. They can eat and drink whatever they choose. They can sleep with whomever they choose. They believe that spiritual persons are liberated from all moral and social norms. Paul recognizes that while Christians may be freed from certain religious and dietary conventions, their freedom is intended to support the community, especially its most vulnerable and impressionable members. Further, given Paul's holistic vision of human life, he believes that what we do with our bodies shapes our spiritual lives, and our spiritual lives shape the quality of our embodiment. Our calling is to glorify God in our bodies, because our bodies are the temple of God (I Corinthians 6:12-20).

Paul believes that both groups share a common characteristic. Their focus on the body as the primary reality puts both Christian freedom and the well-being and unity of the community in jeopardy. While Paul is not a legalist, who demands strict obedience to rules, or an ascetic, who scorns the flesh, he subordinates our desires, values, and lifestyle to the well-being of less mature Christians and the harmony of the church.

QUESTIONS FOR DISCUSSION

1. Consider Paul's image of the Christian life as being similar to running a race. What is the goal of the Christian journey? What are the challenges of running a spiritual marathon?
2. Paul speaks of looking toward the goal and forgetting what lies in the past. What do you think Paul is talking about? What do you need to let go of to be faithful to Christ?
3. People joke that the most often quoted phrase in congregational life is "we've always done it this way." What old tradi-

tions does the church need to de-emphasize or jettison completely to respond to the current age? What does your congregation need to change to be faithful in your community?

4. Looking at your life, what persons do you hold up as worthy of imitation? What characteristics are worthy of imitation?

5. Looking at your life, who have been your mentors? What was special about their relationship with you? How did their mentoring change your life?

6. In I Corinthians 6:20 Paul counsels, "glorify God in your bodies." What does that counsel mean? How might your church support people in the practice of glorifying God in peoples' physical lives?

EXERCISE

Consider the issue of spiritual imitation as it relates to your vocation as a Christian. If people imitated your faith, what would they find helpful? What might be problematic? In what ways does the imitation of Christ shape your walk as a Christian? Take time to examine the model you present to the world, its authenticity, and ways you can be a more faithful model of Christian living.

THEOLOGICAL/SPIRITUAL REFLECTION

The Christian faith has been described as a "race," "pilgrim's progress," "purpose driven," and as a "holy adventure." Take some time to review your life, taking note of the following events, either in a time line or meditative journal:

–   "The hour you first believed," when grace and forgiveness became realities for you.

–   "God encounters" on the way. Special moments when God was truly real in your life.

–   Spiritual crises, or moments of doubt and questioning, when God seemed absent.

- Times of grief and desolation, and how you experienced God at such times.
- Healing moments, when you experienced God's life-transforming touch.
- Pivotal encounters with persons who became your mentor.

Consider the values that guided your journey as well as the temptations you experienced on the way. Toward what goals do you feel God is guiding you today. In what ways can you be faithful to God's vision for your life.

CLOSING PRAYER:

In light of reflecting on your own "race" of faith, take time in silence to give thanks for the God-moments and special persons in your life. If you are in a group, take a few minutes for the group to share these moments and persons following a time of silent reflection.

Loving Creator, we thank you for your presence in every moment of our lives. We thank you that your word – your presence in inspiration, encounter, and scripture – has been – and always be – a lamp unto our feet. We thank you for all the persons you have placed in our lives, whose commitment and care have given us faith and insight for the journey. Help us, O God, to share the graces we have received, as mentors and guides for others along the holy adventure of faith. In Christ's Name. Amen.

NOTES

_____

_____

_____

_____

LESSON 8:
SPIRITUAL PRACTICES FOR PILGRIMS

VISION

Participants will reflect and learn spiritual practices for personal and congregational growth. They will discover the importance of spiritual disciplines for facing life's challenges as well as for nurturing the mind of Christ. In particular, they will learn practices for spiritual growth such as spiritual affirmations, meditative prayer, and prayers of thanksgiving and healing. Participants will be invited to embody two key Pauline phrases, "I can do all things through God who strengthens me" and "My God will supply all your needs."

OPENING PRAYER:

Begin with silent prayer, opening to divine guidance and inspiration. Consider your greatest needs at this time of your life. Reflect on what it means to say "My God will supply all your needs." Claim this statement as being directed to you personally and to your congregation as a community of faith. If you are in a group, take a few moments to lift up the needs of the community as a part of the prayer.

God of abundant life, you have shown us the way, the truth, and the life; you have given us strength in weakness and insight in times of confusion. We lift up our needs and the needs of the community to you. Help us to trust your promises – that you will supply all our needs and that in your strength, we can respond to all of the challenges of livingand dying. Help us to know that you are always near, coming to us in each moment and gathering us into your realm in the hour of our death. Bless us that we may out of this abundance bless others. In Jesus' name. Amen.

READING: PHILIPPIANS 4:1-23

Read Philippians 4:1-23, circling key words and phrases, considering why they are important to you. What is their meaning for your life today?

Then, quietly reflect on Philippians 4:4-9 in the spirit of *lectio divina*. What words or images emerge for you? In what ways might these words shape your spiritual life?

LESSON

EVERYONE MATTERS (4:2-3)

The apostle Paul sees the body of Christ as a living, breathing organism, animated by the spirit of Christ. We are the cells and organs, while Christ is the mind permeating every part. The health of the whole depends on the integrity and health of the parts, and the health of the parts depends on the overall well-being of the whole organism. As Paul says in I Corinthians 12:26: "If one member suffers, all suffer together with it; if one member is honored, all rejoice together with it."

From this perspective, the relationship of Euodia and Syntyche is essential to the well-being of the body. We can suspect that in the Philippian church, where women played significant leadership roles, their current disagreement is undermining the health and mission of the church. We are not told about the source of their conflict, and that is good news, because it allows us to recognize that regardless of the issues involved, unresolved conflict hurts congregations and needs to be prayerfully and publicly addressed. Many congregations are conflict avoidant, just hoping, quite unrealistically, that conflicts will go away on their own without being addressed. Other congregations self-destruct due to divisive conflicts over worship, lifestyle, ethics, theology, and leadership style. These churches fight, but they don't fight fair. They fail to realize that conflicts need to be addressed in ways that enable people in love for one another and congregations to experience greater vitality and vision.

It takes a village to raise a child, support families, nurture effective ministry, and respond to conflicts. Accordingly, Paul calls for a faithful congregational leader to mediate between Euodia and Syntyche. Her or his goal is to achieve common ground and purpose between them, and remind them about the goal of having the mind of Christ. Paul's "loyal companion" will need to encourage them to forgive, to let go of the past, to awaken them to their unity of purpose in Christ.

Paul's words ring true for our time of religious and theological culture wars. We need to pray for those with whom we disagree, pray for our pastors and congregational leaders, and pray that we might address contrasting points of view in the church with grace and forgiveness.

LIFE TRANSFORMING SPIRITUAL PRACTICES (4:4-7)

I must begin with a confession. Philippians 4, especially verses 4-9, 13, 19, is among my favorite passages in scripture. Paul presents the vision of Christ growing within us, producing a harvest of righteousness in chapter one; follows that vision with a description of Christ's universal and sacrificial love and the call and response of grace and intentionality in chapter two; and describes the adventure of faith as a race guided by the hope of intimately knowing Christ in chapter three. Chapter four provides the practices that enable us to experience our vocation as Christ's beloved and growing children, companions in God's mission to heal the earth.

Once again, Paul begins with the invitation to "rejoice." With emphasis Paul proclaims, "Rejoice in the Lord always, again I will say rejoice." Joy is grounded in the sense of God's nearness. For Paul, God's nearness involved both presence and hope. The Philippians are called to live out of their sense of the omnipresence of God right now. God is able, God is faithful, and God is here. Paul affirms that regardless of the challenges of life, God will give us everything we need to live faithfully and joyfully in this life with the hope that nothing – not even death and suffering – can separate us from God's everlasting love. The future and present alike are in God's care and guided by divine inspiration.

Paul's list of spiritual practices for pilgrims is not meant to be exhaustive, but a commitment to any of these will transform your life.

– **Gentleness** – a commitment to self-awareness in your relationships, seeking to love and support everyone we meet. Gentleness involves a life of blessing in which we seek to bless everyone we meet and resolve conflicts in caring and honest ways.

– **Equanimity** – in contrast to anxiety, live calmly with a sense of perspective. Perhaps, Paul is remembering Jesus' words from the Sermon on the Mount, "do not worry about your life, what you will eat, or what you will drink, or your body, what you will wear. ... Consider the lilies of the field, how they grow .... Your heavenly Father knows that you need all these things. But strive first for God's kingdom and God's righteousness and all these things will be given to you as well" (Matthew 6, 25, 28, 32-33).

– **Prayer and supplication** – connecting with God through praise, petition, and intercession. As Paul says in I Thessalonians 5:17, "pray without ceasing." Paul counsels, "let your requests be made known to God." Here we are not providing God with new information, for the One to whom all hearts are open and all desires known is more aware of our needs than we are. When we share our concerns with God, we discover that we are not alone and that we have resources beyond our imagination.

– **Thanksgiving** – connecting with God by counting your blessings, remembering the goodness of being alive and the joy of sharing in God's holy adventure in your life. Those who are thankful always have resources regardless of their economic or external condition.

Spiritual practices such as these are the foundation for experiencing "the peace of God which surpasses all understanding." The peace of God guards our hearts and minds; it protects us from negativity, fear, and chaos, and awakens us to a sense of God's care and protection.

THE POWER OF AFFIRMATIVE FAITH (4:8-9)

The King James translation of Proverbs 23: 7 proclaims, "as a man thinketh in his heart, so is he" (KJV). While this is a contested translation, its historical impact has been significant throughout history. It implies that what we think about, the focus and orientation of our thoughts, shapes who we are and who we will become. The apostle Paul captures this same sentiment in his admonition, "Think about these things." Our thoughts are food for the soul – will we nurture the soul with healthy and life-supportive soul food or unsatisfying spiritual fast food?

Having a positive vision is essential to our spiritual health and personal well-being. Nathaniel Hawthorne tells the legend of a young boy, name Ernest, who grew up spending his days admiring the Great Stone Face, the Old Man of the Mountain, in New Hampshire. To young Ernest, the legendary Stone Face was a wonder of the world. His admiration grew when his mother told him of an ancient prophecy, foretelling that someday there would be a person whose face and character would match the integrity of the Old Man of the Mountain. Inspired by the legend, Ernest spent his lifetime looking for the one person whose character matched the mountain. He observed politicians, successful business people, and other leading citizens, but he could find no one whose spirit matched the mountain. Over the years, Ernest grew to be a person of great wisdom and gravitas, respected for his virtue and common sense by everyone in the region. Although Ernest was disappointed in his quest to find a person who fulfilled the prophecy, his neighbors noticed something unique about Ernest – over the years, his face and character grew to resemble the Great Stone Face that he had admired.

Paul expresses the same sentiment in Romans 12:2: "be not conformed to this world but be transformed by the renewing of your mind." Christian faith involves constantly transforming our minds, bodies, spirits, and relationships to reflect God's vision for our lives. Paul challenges us to focus on "whatever is true, whatever is honorable, whatever is pure whatever is pleasing, whatever is commendable."

In recent years, psychologists and spiritual guides have discovered the power of affirmations to change our lives. Many of us are governed by negative self-talk that shapes how we view ourselves and the world. Sadly, we learn many of these negative images in our childhood. My wife Kate recalls noticing that a good friend's shoe was well worn, and commented, "There's something wrong with your sole, to which her friend replied – What's wrong with my soul? What have I done wrong?" If our image of God is vengeful, judgmental, and angry, we are likely to be judgmental, fearful, or filled with shame. If our image of God is one who draws strict lines between in and out, saved and unsaved, our theology and behavior are likely to exclude persons with whom we disagree or belong to other denominations or religious traditions. If we see ourselves primarily as sinners, loved in spite of who we are but not really loveable, we are likely to have low self-esteem or worry that God will hate us if we step out of line. On the other hand, if we see God as relational, patient, and constantly working in our lives, we will be hopeful, patient, and forgiving of our own and others' imperfections.

Think for a moment of your self-imposed limitations. Are they realistic or are they reflections of low self-esteem or negative and limiting thoughts? Jesus lived out the power of affirmative faith: he affirmed that his mission was to bring abundant life. Accordingly, he lived by a deeper realism grounded in God's love, power, and energy. Jesus lived in an open system in which five loaves and two fish could feed a multitude, prostitutes could become lovers, deniers could become disciples, and persecutors, like Paul, become evangelists. Jesus said to his disciples and to us, "you are the light of the world." In other words, when you open to Christ's ways, you have possibilities beyond your wildest dreams.

GOD'S RESOURCES FOR EVERY SITUATION (4:10-14)

Philippians 4:10-14 reflect Paul's overall peace of mind as well as his confidence in God's trustworthiness. After expressing his gratitude for their gifts, Paul expresses his contentment in life situation. His peace of mind is not the result of good or ill fortune, but his relationship with God. He makes a startling affirmation: "I can do all things through God who strengthens me."

A friend of mine who lives with a chronic and debilitating illness uses Paul's affirmation as her image of hope. While she doesn't expect miracles, this affirmation enables her to believe that God will give her the strength and courage to face everything that comes her way. Over the years, she has achieved more than anyone expected and has, despite her physical limitations, enjoyed an abundant life. This passage came alive for me following an unexpected downsizing from my seminary administrative position. As I repeated this affirmation throughout the day, I was reminded that I have all the resources, creativity, and courage to face the future, knowing that God's resources are infinite and constantly flowing into my life.

GOD WILL SUPPLY YOUR NEEDS (4:15-20)

Philippians 4:15-20 continues Paul's vision of divine abundance as the inspiration for an affirmative and world-transforming faith. Paul once more expresses his gratitude for the Philippians generosity. They stand out among the churches in generosity. But, Paul also recognizes that their gifts in no way compromise his authority as a spiritual teacher. Regardless of their level of support, Paul must have the freedom to share the gospel with integrity and honesty, even if his language is critical. In Mediterranean culture, every gift required some sort of reciprocity. The receiver was considered an inferior, beholden to the giver. Paul takes another path. Paul believes that we live in a circle of giving and receiving, grounded in the reality that all good gifts come from God. We are not owners, but stewards of God's abundant generosity. Our calling is to let God's gifts flow through us to others. We give to others with no expectation of return or no need for reciprocation. In the body of Christ, gifts like grace come with no strings attached.

Paul's positive faith is reflected in his trust that "God will satisfy every need of yours according to his riches in glory in Christ Jesus." Paul, we may suspect, is addressing the Philippians' economic and political situation. Some may have suffered job loss or persecution as a result of following the way of Jesus. Still, Paul's confidence is in God's abundance and God's willingness to give us what we really need, sufficient for every life situation. God is on our side. God wants us to prosper and succeed. This is not individualism or a form of the prosperity gospel in which positive thinking always insures a reward, but a realistic affirmation that regardless of what happens in life, God is with us. In the words of Romans 8:28, "in all things God works for good." Paul also recognizes that in authentic Christian community, no one goes hungry, lacks personal support, and goes without adequate health care. When we care for one another, we all have what we need.

A FINAL WORD (4:21-23)

We don't know if Paul ever visited Philippi again. That was surely his intent. But, whether or not, he returned to this faithful congregation, Paul's words echo through the ages. Paul's egalitarian faith made it possible for descendents of these Gentiles, including the majority of today's readers, to hear the good news of the crucified and risen savior.

Paul's farewell resonates throughout history. The gospel is found in this one sentence, "the grace of our Lord Jesus be with your spirit." When we experience God's grace, we have everything we need – the good work God has begun in our lives will come to fruition and it will be a harvest of righteousness.

QUESTIONS FOR DISCUSSION

1. Imaginatively enter into the first century world of the Philippian church. Consider the relationship of Eudoia and Syntyche. Because this is an imaginative exercise, let your mind expand – you don't have to worry about historical accuracy. What work can you imagine these two women sharing in the founding of the Philippian church? What conflict alienated them from each other? What impact did their disagreement have on the Philippian church? If you were Paul's "loyal companion," how would you go about resolving the situation?

2. Have you ever experienced conflict in the church? How can Christians more creatively and sensitively respond to congregational conflicts? In light of Philippians 4:5, what role might gentleness play in the resolving conflict in church, home, and office?

3. Turning to Philippians 4:4, what does Paul man when he says "rejoice in God always?" What enables us to rejoice in difficult times?

4. Take a moment to read Philippians 4:8-9, considering the following questions:
    –   Looking at today's commercials, what do commercials want you to "think" about? Are the values in commercials a help or hindrance to peoples' faith?
    –   What are your favorite Christian affirmations? (Positive statements stated in the present tense, such as "I am the light of the world" or "God will supply your needs.")
    –   What negative self-talk do you and others use? In what ways can you transform your negative self-talk into positive, life-transforming talk?
    –   Can churches also use negative and positive self-talk? What words describe your congregation's current self-talk? What spiritual affirmation do you need to embody as a congregation?

5. Pause awhile to meditate on Philippians 4:13 and 4:19, listening for God's promises in these passages.

   – What does it mean to believe that "I can do all things through Christ who strengthens me?" What things do you and your congregation need to do to respond to the challenges of your situation? Do we place unnecessary limitations on what we can do and what God can do in our lives? What "miracles" might emerge if we fully trusted God?

   – What does it mean for God to supply all your needs? What are your deepest needs? What are your congregation's greatest needs? What would it mean for your congregation to affirm this spiritual truth? What would it mean for you to affirm this spiritual truth?

6. Paul describes the possibility that we might experience a peace that surpasses understanding. How do you understand spiritual peace? Can you experience peace in the midst of conflict? What are the characteristics of spiritual peace?

7. In Philippians 4:15-20 Paul considers the relationship between a spiritual leader and her or his congregation or supporters. He believes that a pastor must be true to her or his convictions and understanding of the gospel, regardless of the viewpoint of the majority of the congregation. At times a pastor needs to be a prophet, who clearly differentiates her or his message from the norms of the community. (For example, opposing apartheid or segregation; challenging dishonest business practices or willful environmental destruction; speaking out against sexism or racism.) As you consider issues of pastoral authority, reflect on the following questions:

   – In what areas do pastors often differ from their congregations? Have you had pastors and congregants differ on important questions? How did the congregants respond?

- What is the pastor's responsibility when he or she differs from the norms of her or his community, or holds an unpopular position on an issue in politics, theology, ethics, and lifestyle?
- How should congregations respond to a pastor's prophetic word when it challenges long-held norms in the congregation or community?

EXERCISE

In the spirit of the Questions for Discussion, consider the limits that you place on yourself. Do you expect too little from God and from yourself? What great things might you do or experience if you let go of any self-imposed limits?

Take a moment to imagine God's limitless energy flowing through the universe and your life. Imagine yourself achieving great things through God who moves through your life.

THEOLOGICAL/SPIRITUAL REFLECTION

Philippians, chapter four, focuses on practices for the spiritual journey. Spiritual practices reflect God's grace moving through our lives. God is always seeking abundant life for us, but often we are closed to the gifts God wishes to give us. Practices are one way we open to grace and abundance. They connect us with God spiritually, emotionally, mentally, and relationally. Spiritual practices may literally transform our thoughts and our environment. When our perspective on life changes, our interpretation of the world also changes. New possibilities for action emerge. Paul's intent is for the Philippians and us to experience God as a living reality, sufficient to inspire a lifestyle of mission and sacrifice on behalf of Christ.

As you consider the practices described in Philippians 4:4-9, with which practices do you feel most comfortable? What new practices of faith do you wish to try in the future?

CLOSING PRAYER:

God of abundant love, you give us more than we ask for or imagine, yet sometimes we are stuck in our world of individualism and scarcity. Wake us up to your abundant life. Open our hearts and hands so that we may constantly give and receive love, and allow ourselves to be your channels of blessing. Help us to expect more of you in our lives and more of ourselves as we seek to be your faithful companions in healing the world. In Jesus' name. Amen.

NOTES

_____

_____

_____

_____

_____

_____

_____

_____

_____

_____

BIBLIOGRAPHY

Barth, Karl. *Epistle to the Philippians*. Philadelphia: Westminster/John Knox, 2002.

Bassler, Jouette. *Navigating Paul: An Introduction to Key Theological Concepts*. Louisville: Westminster/John Knox, 2007

Bassler, Jouette. *Pauline Theology: Thessalonians, Philippians, Galatians, Philemon*. Atlanta: Society of Biblical Literature, 2002.

Beardslee, William. *A House for Hope: A Study in Process and Biblical Thought*. Philadelphia: Westminster Press, 1972.

Borg, Marcus and John Dominic Crossan. *The First Paul: Reclaiming the Radical Visionary Behind the Church's Conservative Icon*. San Francisco: Harper One, 2009.

Bruce, F.F. *Philippians*. Peabody, MA: Hendrickson, 1989.

Boring, Eugene and Fred Craddock. *The People's New Testament Commentary*. Louisville: Westminster/John Knox, 2009.

Cornwall, Robert D. *Ephesians: A Participatory Study Guide*. Gonzalez, FL: Energion Publications, 2010.

Craddock, Fred. *Philippians*. Atlanta: John Knox, 1985.

Dunn, James. *The New Perspective on Paul*. Grand Rapids: Eerdmans, 2007.

Dunn, James. *The Theology of Paul the Apostle*. Grand Rapids: Eerdmans, 2006.

Epperly, Bruce. *God's Touch: Faith, Wholeness, and the Healing Miracles of Jesus*. Louisville: Westminster/John Knox, 2001.

Epperly, Bruce. *Holy Adventure: 41 Days of Audacious Living*. Nashville: Upper Room, 2008.

Farmer, Ronald. *Beyond the Impasse: The Promise of a Process Hermeneutic*. Macon, GA: Mercer University Press, 1996.

Fee, Gordon. *Paul's Letter to the Philippians*. Grand Rapids: Eerdmans, 1995.

Fowl, Stephen. *Philippians*. Grand Rapids: Eerdmans, 2005.

Hawthorne, Gerald. *Philippians*. New York: Thomas Nelson, 2004.

Metzger, Bruce. *The Text of the New Testament*. New York: Oxford University Press, 1992.

O'Brien, Peter. *The Epistle to the Philippians: A Commentary on the Greek Text*. Grand Rapids: Eerdmans, 1991.

Carolyn Oseik, *Philippians and Philemon*. Nashville: Abingdon, 2000.

Peterson, Eugene. *The Message: The Bible in Contemporary Language*. Colorado Springs, CO: NavPress, 2007.

Sanders, E.P. *Paul: A Very Short Introduction*. New York: Oxford University Press, 2007.

Williamson, Clark. *Has God Rejected His People?* Nashville: Abingdon, 1982.

Wright, N.T.. *Justification: God's Plan and Paul's Vision*. Downers Grove: Intervarsity, 2009.

Wright, N.T. *Paul for Everyone: The Prison Letters – Ephesians, Philippians, Colossians, and Philemon*. Louisville: Westminster/John Knox, 2004.

Wright, N.T. *Paul: In Fresh Perspective*. Minneapolis: Fortress Press, 2009.

APPENDIX A:
PARTICIPATORY STUDY METHOD

HOW CAN I GET MORE FROM MY BIBLE READING?

Although the Bible is a timeless source of inspiration and creativity, there is no shortcut in Bible study. Scripture invites us to be part of the dialogue between God and the world, in which God's invites us to be partners in healing the earth and its peoples. If you want to be part of this ongoing process of call and response, you have to take the time to dig deeply and prayerfully to discover God's word of grace and healing amid the words of scripture.

There are some things you can do to help you experience the Bible as a living word addressed to you and your congregation. In this appendix you will find a pathway to Bible study that can transform your life, spiritually and intellectually. (I am grateful to the insights of Henry Neufeld and Robert Cornwall that serve as the foundation for the appendices.)

PREPARATION

As you explore Paul's Letter to the Philippians, here are some tools for personal transformation:

1. **Gather Materials** — have pen, paper, highlighters or other markers and all materials you will need for study available. I have found that jotting insights down as I go along increases my understanding of the text and enables me to gather these insights weeks and months later.

2. **Conditions** — Find a place where you can study. This can be your sacred space, or altar for personal transformation, what the Celtic Christians described as "thin places," where God meets humanity in saving ways. If you study well with music playing, put

some on. If you prefer quiet, arrange for a quiet place for reflection.

3. **Resources** — Get a small, theologically-sound set of study materials that reflect both your own and other faith positions. For suggestions see the resource list in appendix B.

4. **Prayer**

As you begin your study, consider the premise that scripture comes to us as God-breathed or inspired, and therefore it is "useful for teaching for reproof, for correction, and for training in righteousness, so that everyone who belongs to God may be proficient, equipped for every good work" (2 Timothy 3:1 6-17). Keeping in mind this word, share in this prayer:

Loving and eternal God, in the reading of the scripture, may your word be heard; in the meditations of our hearts, may your word be known; and in the faithfulness of our lives, may your word be shown.

In hearing your word, may we be transformed, and in so doing, become your partners in transforming the world. In Jesus' Name. Amen.

(Adapted from Chalice Worship, 384).

GET AN OVERVIEW OF THE PASSAGE

Read the passage multiple times. Memorizing is useful, at least of key texts. (This will also require you to select key texts.) Read from different Bible versions to deepen your encounter with the text open up different ways of understanding the passage. At this point don't use commentaries, study notes, your concordance, or anything which takes your concentration off of the passage you are studying. While other peoples' understandings are important, you need to claim scripture as a personal word addressed to you. Simply open to God's inspiration emerging from your own experience. God is speaking in your life. Let God's wisdom soak deeply in body, mind, and spirit. In this spirit, you may choose to do the imaginative or *lectio divina* exercises described throughout this book.

STUDY THE BACKGROUND OF THE TEXT

As you study the text, ask the following questions: who wrote the passage, to whom it was written, what is the situation being addressed, and what type of literature it is.

REFLECT, QUESTION, RESEARCH, COMPARE

Reflect on the passage. If you are having difficulty identifying with the text, think about telling someone else about the passage, such as a friend in need of encouragement, someone who is struggling with their faith or asking questions about faith, or a child for whom no question is silly or unimportant.

Consider: What questions might they ask about this passage? You can formulate thought questions or fact questions. Fact questions focus on what the author is actually saying in her or his time and place. Thought questions may lead you to other revelations that lay well beyond the author's intention in the passage. You are part of shaping the biblical tradition in your time, making it come alive as good news in our world.

You might consider creating an outline of the passage, comparing it with other scriptures or with the writings of figures in church history, or spiritual leaders today (such as Billy Graham, the Pope, Mother Teresa, Dorothy Day, Martin Luther King, Howard Thurman, or even non-Christians such as the Dalai Lama.)

Ask: What similar experiences are we having today? Could this help me better understand the passage. For example, if you have had a vision or mystical experience in which God truly became real for you, this might help you understand the vision, recorded Ezekiel 1 or Isaiah 6 or Paul's vision of a Macedonian man, beckoning him to come to Philippi.

Ask your friends about experiences they have had of God's presence. When did God become more than a word to them?

You might consult historical figures such as: Columba, Teresa of Avilla, Julian of Norwich, Augustine, Martin Luther, John Wesley, John Calvin, Walter Rauschenbusch, Paul Tillich, Dietrich Bonhoeffer, Reinhold Niebuhr, and many others.

SHARE YOUR THOUGHTS

Ask yourself how this text relates to your experience. After claiming your insights, share your understanding with another person in a dialogical give and take in which both of you are open to new insights on the meaning of the text. Get to know the person with whom you are sharing. Share your experience of faith and then the text's meaning for you. Always work from your own personal experience with God, including your doubts, questions, hopes, and dreams. Be honest in your conversation about questions and struggles you are having with the scriptural passage. Store up the experiences your friends share with you to use in studying further scripture. The purpose of sharing is not just to help others through your own insights. It is also intended to provide you with new insights and ways of understanding scripture.

Paul's Letter to the Philippians was intended for a community of faith. Sharing helps keep you a part of the community. Make sure that some of your sharing is with people who have experience and training in scripture, theology, and spiritual formation, including people with different theological perspectives or spiritual experiences. This will help you go beyond superficial and parochial understandings of scripture and deepen your sense of God's presence in the many varieties of Christian experience.

EXAMPLE PASSAGE

1 Kings 19:11-18

1. Begin your study with silent reflection and prayer.
2. Read the passage several times in the spirit of lectio divina or holy reading. What words or images speak to you today?
3. Reflect on Elijah's mystical experience.
   - How does Elijah respond to God?
   - What is God's intention in appearing to Elijah?.

- How did Elijah know the Lord was not in the wind, the earthquake or the fire? Can God appear in such dramatic events?
- Does God respond to Elijah's complaint? Have you had similar experiences?
- Have you ever had a life-transforming experience of God's reality and intentions for your life?
- Is Elijah as much alone as he feels he is? Or are there others who remain faithful to God? (No, there are 7,000 more faithful people, v. 18.)
- What other Biblical characters have experienced something similar to this? (Daniel 3:1-30 — the fiery furnace; Acts 9:1-9, the apostle Paul on the Road to Damascus)
- Have you experienced similar feelings? Have you ever felt completely alone in your faith? Have you ever suffered for your faith or ethics?
- Share your experiences!! And, listen with openness and affirmation to others' faith experiences? God speaks through others' experiences to deepen our own faith.

PRAYER

Conclude with silence, listening to God's sighs too deep for words. Listen for places in your life in need of healing and transformation.

Holy One, open my heart and mind to your creative transformation. By your grace, let me be a new creation, open to your inspiration and willing to follow where you lead. You are the way, the truth, and the life, not just for me but for all creation. Help me to experience you working in my life, but also in those whose spiritual pathways differ from mine. Like Elijah, let me experience you in the small as well as the great, the simple as well as the dramatic. Be with me in times of celebration and doubt, as I seek to be faithful to you. Let your mission be mine as I seek to be your companion in healing the world. In Jesus' name. Amen.

APPENDIX B
TOOLS FOR LIFE-TRANSFORMING BIBLE STUDY

The following are some suggested resources for Bible study. These will help you join head with heart and hands.

BIBLE VERSIONS

You will need a Bible version that you can understand without having to consult an English dictionary too often.

√ For quick reading (overview):

— *Contemporary English Version* (CEV)
Quite accessible; high degree of accuracy within the context of its aim for easy readability.

— *The Cotton Patch Version* by Clarence Jordan
An interpretive paraphrase reflecting the dialect and culture of rural Georgia. It reminds us that God comes to us in terms of our concrete experience and not some abstract, timeless world. Its Southern flavor also provides an interracial vision of scripture, often missed in translations.

— *The Message* by Eugene Peterson
Heavily paraphrased with cultural terms translated. This version is fun to read, and enables us to experience God's voice in the voices of North American Christians. However, it tends to obscure the unique elements of the original cultures.

— *New Living Translation* (NLT)
A more accurate re-visioning of the Living Bible. This is the easy-reading Bible aimed at evangelical Christians.

- *Today's New International Version*
  Shows its relationship to the popular NIV in many wordings, but uses simplified language and sentence structure in many cases.

√   For study or reading:

- *Common English Bible* (CEB)
  A new translation sponsored by mainline or moderate Protestant publishing houses, the CEB attempts to combine high level scholarship with readability.
- *New International Version* (NIV)
  The NIV is a dynamic equivalent translation of the Bible that is popular among evangelical Christians.
- *New Revised Standard Version* (NRSV)
  An updating of the Revised Standard Version, it is the Bible of choice for mainline or moderate/progressive Christians needing a study Bible. It is known for its attempt to use gender neutral language where appropriate.
- *Revised English Bible* (REB)
  This version was translated by an interdenominational/ecumenical committee with interfaith review that exhibits the different texture of British English.
- *New American Standard Bible* (NASB)
  A very formal rendering of the original languages, the NASB has its roots in conservative evangelicalism.

STUDY BIBLES

Study Bibles usually contain introductory articles giving the Biblical context, information on methodology and overviews of various themes in the Bible. They will also include introductions to each book and comments on difficult passages. Study Bibles will reflect religious views of editors and authors, some more than others.

√ *New Interpreter's Study Bible* (NRSV)
   This new study Bible includes extensive historical and theological annotations, good introductions and outlines, and excursuses giving further background and insight regarding particular themes and passages.

√ *New Oxford Annotated Bible* (NRSV)
   A standard scholarly study Bible, often used in universities and seminaries.

√ *HarperCollins Study Bible* (NRSV)
   Carrying the sponsorship of the academic Society of Biblical Literature, it has notes from a mainstream or liberal perspective acknowledgment of more conservative options.

√ *The NIV Study Bible* (Zondervan)
   Popular among evangelicals, bringing a more conservative approach to Biblical interpretation and study.

BIBLE HANDBOOKS

Bible handbooks provide historical and cultural information, usually with a number of general articles and then comments on particular books and passages. Using a Bible handbook along with your Bible is like having a Bible with study notes, though usually having a handbook in a separate volume will mean that the handbook contains more exhaustive information. Bible handbooks, like study Bibles, will reflect religious presuppositions of the editors.

√ Mainstream and/or Liberal
   – *The Cambridge Companion to the Bible*
   – *Oxford Companion to the Bible*

√ Moderate
   – *Eerdman's Handbook to the Bible*

√ Conservative
   – *Zondervan Handbook to the Bible*

BIBLE COMMENTARIES

Bible commentaries are designed to provide introductions, background, and interpretation of biblical texts. They come in many forms, ranging from one–volume efforts to commentaries on individual books.

√ Mainstream
- *New Interpreter's Bible*, 12 volumes (Abingdon)
  An updating of the venerable Interpreter's Bible, this is a mainstream commentary set drawing its authors from across the Christian community, including evangelical, mainline, Catholic, and Orthodox scholars.
- *New Interpreter's One Volume Commentary* (Abingdon)
  Based on the principles of the much larger multi–volume edition, it is a completely new commentary and not simply an abridgement.
- *HarperCollins Bible Commentary* (HarperOne)
  As with the HarperCollins Bible Dictionary, this commentary is sponsored by the Society of Biblical Literature.
- *People's New Testament Commentary of the New Testament* (WJK Press)
  This commentary on the New Testament is written by two Disciples of Christ scholars, Fred Craddock and Eugene Boring.
- *The New Jerome Bible Commentary*, 3rd edition (Prentice Hall)
  This is a predominantly Roman Catholic commentary, authored and edited by highly regarded critical scholars.

√ Evangelical
- *Eerdmans Commentary on the Bible*
  This work is very compatible with mainstream scholarship, but comes from a publisher that stands as a bridge between evangelical and mainline Protestantism.

- *New Bible Commentary: 21st Century edition* (IVP)
  A thorough and accessible commentary, written by some
  of the leading evangelical bible scholars.

BIBLE CONCORDANCES

Concordances may be exhaustive, complete, or concise. In
addition they may either be either organized by words or topics.
Many Bibles contain small, concise concordances. Many study
Bibles contain topical concordances. Exhaustive concordances
contain every reference to a word listed under every word.
Complete concordances contain references to each and every verse,
using significant terms, though not necessarily under every word
in the verse. Concise concordances contain selective references and
may not reference all verses. Topical concordances provide a guide
to topics covered by specific texts. This can be helpful, but one
must always remember that unlike a typical concordance, which is
rooted in word usage, this type is more likely to be driven by
theological presuppositions.

Concordances with Greek and/or Hebrew Lexicons
(dictionaries or vocabularies) can be useful, but one should
remember that translation is not as simple as just picking a word
from a dictionary definition. Context always determines usage and
meaning.

√   Exhaustive with Greek/Hebrew
  - *Strong's Exhaustive Concordance.*
    It is part of the public domain and is regularly reprinted.
    It is based on the King James Version and an older
    lexicon. It's numbering system and lexicon has served as
    the model for other concordances.
  - *The NIV Exhaustive Concordance* (Zondervan)
    Based completely on the NIV, it goes beyond Strong's.
  - *New American Standard Exhaustive Concordance of the
    Bible/Hebrew–Aramaic and Greek Dictionaries*

- *New American Standard Strong's Exhaustive Concordance*
  Based on the *Strong's Concordance* system, it is keyed to the *NASB.*

√ *Exhaustive Concordances*
- *NRSV Concordance Unabridged (Zondervan)*
  Keyed to the NSRV.

√ *Complete Concordances*
- *Cruden's Complete Concordance to the KJV.*
  This is an 18th century product, but because it is public domain it is regularly reprinted.

√ Concise Concordances
- *The Concise Concordance to the New Revised Standard Version* (Oxford)

√ Topical Concordances
- *Holman Concise Topical Concordance* (Holman Reference)
- *TopicalAnalysis of the Bible* (Baker)

BIBLE DICTIONARIES

Bible dictionaries provide definitions of various biblical terms, information about places and people, and introductory information about biblical books. Most information contained in a Bible handbook can be found in a Bible dictionary, but it will be organized much differently.

The religious views of authors and editors will impact the content of a Bible dictionary, as it does with a handbook or commentary. When purchasing a Bible dictionary, it is always best to find one that has been authored/edited by reputable scholars, and is current and even–handed in its approach.

√ *Mainstream*
- *HarperCollins Bible Dictionary*, Revised Edition. (HarperOne)
- *A Dictionary of the Bible*, 2nd ed. (Oxford University Press)

Based upon the Harper-Collins Bible Dictionary, this is a more up–to–date expansion.
- *Anchor Bible Dictionary,* 6 volumes (Doubleday)
- *Eerdman's Dictionary of the Bible*
- *New Interpreter's Dictionary of the Bible,* 5 volumes, (Abingdon)

√ Evangelical
- *New International Bible Dictionary* (Zondervan)
- *New Bible Dictionary,* 3rd edition. (Intervarsity Press)
- *Zondervan Encyclopedia of the Bible,* Revised Edition (5 volumes)

BIBLE ATLASES

Bible atlases contain maps and related background materials that assist students of the bible placing texts and individuals in their proper historical and geographical context.

It is important once again to stress the need for up–to–date reference works. It is also important to note that theology impacts the results of the work– knowing the theological orientation of a publisher can be helpful in this. Therefore, Harper–Collins is probably more mainstream and cross–confessional, while IVP and Zondervan will be more evangelical or conservative in perspective.

√ *HarperCollins Concise Atlas of the Bible.* (HarperOne)
  In paperback and at 152 pages, this one may be all the average Bible student needs.
√ *The MacMillan Bible Atlas, 3rd edition.* (MacMillan)
  This has been a standard atlas, which is marked by the editorship of Jewish scholars.
√ *The BiblicalWorld* (National Geographic)
√ *HarperCollins Atlas of Bible History* (HarperOne)
√ *Oxford Bible Atlas* (Oxford University Press)
√ *The IVP Atlas of Bible History.* (IVP)
√ *Zondervan Atlas of the Bible* (Zondervan)

SOME DEFINITIONS

Note: Labels in connection with many of these resources can be misleading. No label is to be regarded as either pejorative or complimentary. "Mainstream" doesn't mean "correct," for example. Labels give us a sense of a book's perspective, although the lines between evangelical and mainstream scholarship are blurring among 21st century scholars.

Mainstream: Materials which would be suitable for use in departments of religion at secular universities, most seminaries, and moderate and progressive Christian congregations. This does not imply more or less correct in content. "Progressive" – like liberal – is hard to define, but involves openness to transformation, the insights of culture and other religious, and the full breadth of God's revelation in human and non-human experience.

Interfaith: Involving persons other than those of one faith (Christians and Jews, for example). Distinguish from interdenominational, or ecumenical, which relate to the Christian community's unity amid diversity.

Evangelical: A high view of biblical authority, with particular emphasis on divine sovereignty and the Lordship of Christ.

Also in the
Participatory Study Series

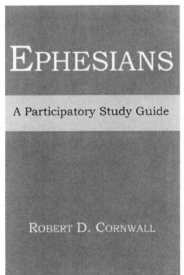

EPHESIANS

A Participatory Study Guide

ROBERT D. CORNWALL

Following the outlines of the Participatory Study Method, Dr. Robert Cornwall presents a study guide to the book of Ephesians that is both usable and challenging while not skirting the difficult issues. These eight lessons take you through the letter leading from the history and background to modern application and sharing in corporate study and worship.

Whether you are approaching this book as an individual, as a small group, or in a larger classroom setting, this study guide will provide you with direction, exercises, and questions for discussion and further investigation.

Geoffrey Lentz and Henry Neufeld, a pastor and a teacher, team up in *Learning and Living Scripture* to present the Participatory Bible Study Method, an approach to Bible study that is rooted in the conviction that God can and will speak to us in scripture.

They bring together their different experiences and perspectives to present this method of study in a practical, usable way.

There are three key elements to this study:

1. The integration of prayer and study
2. Serious questioning and research that is nonetheless within reach of the non-scholar
3. Study in community with both witness and accountability through sharing

In this guide you will learn to integrate prayer and scripture reading while also being faithful to the historical meaning of the text and its use throughout history by the community of faith. This method is not just about study and learning facts; it's about letting the God who gave scripture live in and through you, as you learn and share.

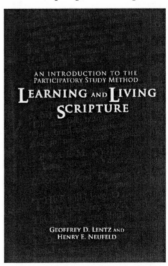

AN INTRODUCTION TO THE
PARTICIPATORY STUDY METHOD

LEARNING AND LIVING
SCRIPTURE

GEOFFREY D. LENTZ AND
HENRY E. NEUFELD

More from Energion Publications

Personal Study

Christianity and Secularism	$16.99
Evidence for the Bible	$16.99
Finding My Way in Christianity	$16.99
Holy Smoke, Unholy Fire	$14.99
The Jesus Paradigm	$17.99
The Messiah and His Kingdom to Come	$19.99
Not Ashamed of the Gospel	$12.99
What's In A Version?	$12.99
When People Speak for God	$17.99

Christian Living

52 Weeks of Ordinary People – Extraordinary God	$7.99
Be an Encourager	$7.99
Daily Devotions of Ordinary People – Extraordinary God	$19.99
Directed Paths	$7.99
Grief: Finding the Candle of Light	$8.99
I Want to Pray	$7.99
Rite of Passage for the Home and Church	$13.99
Soup Kitchen for the Soul	$12.99
Words of Life, Light, and Love	$7.99

Bible Study

Ephesians: A Participatory Study Guide	$9.99
The Gospel According to St. Luke: A Participatory Study Guide	$8.99
Identifying Your Gifts and Service: Small Group Edition	$12.99
Learning and Living Scripture	$12.99
Revelation: A Participatory Study Guide	$9.99
To the Hebrews: A Participatory Study Guide	$9.99
Why Four Gospels?	$11.99

Theology

Christian Archy	$9.99
God's Desire for the Nations	$18.99
Operation Olive Branch	$16.99
Out of This World	$24.99
The Politics of Witness	$9.99
Ultimate Allegiance	$9.99

Fiction

Megabelt	$12.99

Energion Publications

P.O. Box 841 – Gonzalez, FL 32560

Website: http://energionpubs.com

Phone: (850) 525-3916